M000159594

# THE COMPLETE GUIDE TO ENGLISH SPRINGER SPANIELS

Dr. Jo de Klerk

LP Media Inc. Publishing

Text copyright © 2019 by LP Media Inc.

www.lpmedia.org

- - - - - - - - - - - - - - - - - - - - - - - - - - - - - - - - - - - - - -

Publication Data

Dr. Jo de Klerk

The Complete Guide to English Springer Spaniels ---- First edition.

Summary: "Successfully raising an English Springer Spaniel dog from puppy to old age" --- Provided by publisher.

ISBN: 978-1-09669-579-0

[1.English Springer Spaniels --- Non-Fiction] I. Title.

- - - - - - - - - - - - - - - - - - - - - - - - - - - - - - - - - - - - - -

Design by Sorin Rădulescu

First paperback edition, 2019

# TABLE OF CONTENTS

## CHAPTER 18

# ACKNOWLEDGMENTS

*Bluff*

This book is dedicated to the three Springer Spaniels I have had in my life: Bluff, Tosca, and Roxy. Bluff was a sensitive soul that looked over my cot when I was born. I grew up beside her and shared many happy moments with her throughout my childhood years. Losing her when I was 11 years old was the hardest loss of any animal I have had to deal with.

Tosca was hard as nails. She was a typical working-line Springer Spaniel. She was determined, intense, and hyperactive. This dog had two speeds: fast and off. And the off setting never lasted too long. Tosca went blind as she became older, but it didn't stop her. She would still charge around at top speed, to the point at which she had to wear a high-viz jacket printed with the word "blind" when out in public, so that people could understand why a Spaniel had just run into them at top speed.

*Tosca*

*Roxy*

Roxy is the current Spaniel in my life. Unlike the previous Springers, she is shy, sensitive, and timid, until she's out in the countryside, of course. She is more delicate than the other two, and needs to be cuddled far more than any dog I have ever known.

In addition to acknowledging the Springers that have been in my life, in aiding me to write this book, I would also like to extend a massive thank-you to Clare Hardy, my long-time proofreader. Her expertise is second to none, and I appreciate all her help in turning my writing into a fluid, easy-to-read piece of work.

# CHAPTER 1
# Breed Overview

The English Springer Spaniel is one of the world's best loved breeds, and it's not hard to see why. With a long history working in the field alongside their human master, there has always been a very special relationship between man and dog when it comes to the Springer Spaniel. In fact, the bond is so strong that it has become the defining characteristic of the breed, and no other will love you more. The English Springer Spaniel will want to be with you at all times, and will thrive on your attention. But alongside this undivided loyalty, the Springer Spaniel can be rather complex, and so individual that no one Springer is the same as the next!

If you are considering an English Springer Spaniel, this book will introduce you to the breed and provide an overview of how to care for your dog.

Photo Courtesy of
Trevor Kerr
www.trevkerrphotographer.com

# About the Breed

*"Springers make great companions or even therapy dogs. They are very adaptable and can be trained to do almost anything. I have said; The only thing a Springer can't learn is something you don't try to teach them."*

**Randy Huffey**
*Huffey's Springers*

The English Springer Spaniel originated as a hunting breed, but relatively recently in its long history, the breed diverged into the working line and the show line. You will read a lot about this important subdivision in this book, as the distinction in temperament between these two lines is often overlooked. The working Springer is a highly energetic, focused, and prey-driven dog with the athleticism and stamina that make him excel in flushing out game for the hunt. However, he can be rather too intense in a domestic environment, and the more relaxed show-bred (or bench) Springer can make a better pet. Both working and show lines, however, are highly intelligent, very trainable, and completely devoted to their owners. This level of devotion is extremely endearing, and makes for the strongest of bonds, but anyone thinking of getting a Springer needs to understand that they are people dogs, and they cannot cope with long periods alone. However, if you can commit to the emotional neediness of the Springer Spaniel, they will become the most loving and faithful member of your family, eager to please you and quick to learn. In fact, the best company you could ever wish for!

Photo Courtesy of
Megan Wharrie

# Looks

The English Springer Spaniel is almost always either black and white, or brown and white. Brown is termed "liver." Other variants suggest some crossbreeding in the dog's pedigree. The coat is long and silky, especially the show line, which has long feathering. The working Springer has a slightly coarser, shorter coat with less feathering.

The most striking feature of the English Springer Spaniel is his beautiful silky ears. These are longer and more profusely feathered in the show line than the working line. They are set a little higher than the Cocker Spaniel. They frame his expressive brown eyes. The liver and white Springer Spaniel will have a brown or pink nose, and the black and white Springer has a black nose. His coat has large patches of color, and as he matures, flecks of color known as "ticking" will appear. These look like stripes if he has a long coat, or spots on the shorter hair of his legs and if he is clipped.

The English Springer Spaniel is classed as a medium-sized dog. As with all breeds, the male is typically larger than the female at 20 inches in height and 50 pounds. The female averages 19 inches in height and 40 pounds in weight.

*Photo Courtesy of Ally Vande Kopple*

The breed standard differs in every country, and as a result, the appearance of an English Springer Spaniel may not be identical across the world. But as a pedigree dog, an English Springer Spaniel should be bred to their own country's breed standard.

The English Springer Spaniel is usually docked in the USA, especially if he is to be used for showing or hunting. In the UK, docking is illegal, except for working breeds. So an exemption may be granted for the working Springer Spaniel if hunting or other permitted occupations are his designated purpose. The undocked tail of the English Springer Spaniel boasts some long feathering, which it may be argued could get entangled if a dog is working in the field. In practice, the Springer will always proudly bring back an impressive array of sticky burrs in his ears and long tail when out exploring the countryside. The long coat of the English Springer Spaniel needs regular grooming, because apart from attracting undergrowth, it tangles readily and can form mats that pull at the skin and harbor bacteria. Also, Springer Spaniels always find mud and water whenever they are outside.

The English Springer Spaniel is a beautiful dog, which has made the breed universally popular, but those good looks are quite high maintenance. However, this is all part of the fun of owning a Springer Spaniel.

# Age Expectancy

An English Springer Spaniel will typically live for 12-14 years. It is important to consider the future when taking on an English Springer Spaniel, as changes in personal circumstances may occur during this time period. This is especially important with the English Springer Spaniel since it bonds so closely with its owner.

The English Springer Spaniel is predisposed to a fairly high number of health conditions that may affect his natural life expectancy, and these are detailed in Chapter 15. If you are buying a puppy, you can reduce the risk of your dog suffering from a range of genetic conditions by always buying from a registered breeder. In addition, to ensure that your dog lives his allotted years to the maximum, you should provide him with a good quality diet, make sure he is kept at a healthy weight, provide him with plenty of daily exercise, and make sure he has regular veterinary care.

# Personality

*"One of the most unique characteristics of the English Springer Spaniel is their love of humans. Whatever you are doing they want to do with you. They will curl up on the couch with you all day or run and play all day. They are totally unselfish loyal companions."*

**Ahavah Tindell**
*Aquilla Creek Farms*

The temperament of the English Springer Spaniel is defined in the breed standard. The UK breed standard states that he should be friendly and bidable, with a happy disposition, and the American breed standard expands

Photo Courtesy of
Graham Briggs

on the term "biddable" by stating he is eager to please, quick to learn, and willing to obey. The American standard also uses the term "tractability," meaning that he can be easily handled and taught to do a job, which makes him a perfect working dog. It also helps with training the English Springer Spaniel to be a domestic pet and fit into family life.

Both the UK and American breed standards state that aggression and timidity are undesirable in the English Springer Spaniel. Aggression is very uncommon, except in rare cases of "Spaniel Rage," which is a genetic condition sometimes found in show lines. Timidity may be more common as the breed can be quite neurotic; however, sensitive conditioning and socialization at the puppy stage can help develop the desired confidence that a Springer Spaniel should possess. Sadly though, because Springer Spaniels are so sensitive, bad experiences can stay with them for a long time. So, if you are adopting an older dog from a rescue, he may require careful rehabilitation. In some cases, dogs that have suffered psychological damage may never recover fully after being mistreated or neglected. However, the English Springer Spaniel is naturally disposed to form a deep bond with his human. So, whatever has gone on in his past, there is always hope that he will respond to love and consistency, and his trust can be restored.

> **FUN FACT**
> **Color Variations**
>
> English Springer Spaniels come in a wide range of colors. The most common colors seen on these Spaniels' coats are black, liver, and white. In accordance with the breed standard set by the board of directors of the American Kennel Club (AKC), red, orange, or lemon-colored English Springers are outliers.

If there is one thing that the English Springer Spaniel has in spades, it is personality! However, as anyone who has owned the breed will tell you, every Springer is different. They are bursting with character but are all complete individuals. Some may be tough and feisty, others emotional and needy. Some may have inexhaustible energy, others may enjoy lying flat out in the sunshine. Getting to know the complexities of your Springer Spaniel is all a part of the journey. As you get to understand him, his close connection to you means that he is getting to understand you too. The Springer Spaniel is so intelligent and connected that it will seem as if you can read each other's mind as your relationship grows. The term "Man's Best Friend" applies to few breeds more than the English Springer Spaniel.

# Inside the Home

The English Springer Spaniel is a medium sized dog, but his natural exuberance, especially as a puppy, means that he can fill a vastly disproportionate space! So be prepared for your bundle of energy to clear a pathway of chaos through your house, not to mention anything edible left around, as he makes your home his own!

Of course, your English Springer Spaniel does not need to have the run of the entire house, but it is important that he has adequate space in the area in which he is allowed. It is also important to ensure the room is free from anything hazardous, such as breakable objects, gadgets with batteries, even pharmaceuticals and chocolate. Springer Spaniels are energetic dogs, so thinking about how this impacts the household before you bring him home is vital.

Crate training is highly recommended if you are bringing home a puppy, as if your English Springer Spaniel is conditioned to having his own space from an early age, he will never feel restricted by it, but will find it a place of safety. Not only will his crate provide him with a sense of emotional well-being, it will also allow time out for the family from the non-stop exuberance of a puppy, protect the furniture and household objects from being chewed or destroyed, set the ground-rules, and most importantly, provide a firm foundation for housebreaking your puppy.

The English Springer Spaniel is a moderate shedder, especially in the spring and fall, so if you are particularly house proud, you may either have to relax your high standards, or be prepared to vacuum or sweep on a daily basis. Grooming your dog regularly outside in the yard can help prevent shedding inside the home. Your Springer will also bring presents back from his walk, including leaves, burrs, grass, and bits of undergrowth. During the winter months he will also come back with his long coat caked in mud, so he will need showering down regularly, or brushing when the mud is dry.

Carpets, rugs, and fabric upholstery will attract and hold hair; hard surfaces and vinyl or leather upholstery are easier to keep clean when you have an English Springer Spaniel. This is also a consideration when you are busy with housebreaking, as there will inevitably be some accidents.

Probably the most stressful incident that can occur when you share your home with a dog is a flea infestation. Your dog is bound to pick up fleas from contact with other dogs during his lifetime, but the good news is, a monthly spot-on treatment applied to the back of your dog's neck will kill any fleas as soon as they try to feed, ensuring they never become established in your home.

With his shedding undercoat and dander, the English Springer Spaniel is unfortunately not suitable for severe allergy sufferers, so if anyone in the household, or your regular visitors are affected in this way, the Springer Spaniel will not be a good option. On the other hand, studies have shown that children who are brought up with dogs are less likely to suffer allergies later in life (Lemanske, Robert, and Gern, James. *Effects of dog ownership and genotype on immune development and atopy in infancy.* [2004]).

Any dog setting up camp in the family home will bring with him his own special doggy odor. The English Springer Spaniel is not known as a particularly strong-smelling breed; however, his presence will be detectable, especially to visitors. Many owners find their dog's smell endearing, but it is worth considering if it may offend you, as it is not the dog's fault. You may need to shower your Springer Spaniel off after his muddy walks more than most other breeds, especially if he has been true to his Springer instincts and found a stagnant pond, but dogs should not be bathed excessively with shampoo, as it strips the coat of its natural oils. Doggy deodorants are also not recommended as they will only mask the odor, offend your dog, and potentially irritate his skin. However, there are air freshening products on the market that claim to neutralize the odor of dog in the home if this troubles you.

The good news is that English Springer Spaniels are great learners when it comes to housebreaking, so they are less likely than other breeds to soil your house once they have learned to toilet outside.

Once you have considered the impact an English Springer Spaniel will have on your home, and have some coping strategies in place, then there is nothing to beat coming home to a Springer, overjoyed to see you, and bringing you a soggy, chewed slipper in his mouth as a gift that he is sure you will appreciate!

# Outside the Home

It is very important for an active breed such as the English Springer Spaniel to have access to an outdoor space immediately outside his home. For most people, this is their back yard. A private back yard is ideal, because you can make sure that it is safe and enclosed. This provides your Springer Spaniel with an area where he can run around off leash and enjoy exercising his natural instincts, as well as a place for his regular toilet breaks. Housebreaking your Springer Spaniel is discussed in Chapter 6, but having a private yard is a definite advantage, as your dog will identify his preferred toileting spots that makes establishing a regular habit much easier. You also take responsibility for clearing up after your dog in your own space. This is vital if you have young children.

When making your yard secure, certain small breeds may like to dig their way out, and other larger breeds may be more inclined to jump over fences. Your Springer may do both! As a puppy, his escape route may be under the fence, and as an adult it may be over! For this reason, your yard fence needs to come right to the ground, and ideally it should be six feet high. Once your Springer is trained and settled and knows his territory, he is less likely to stray. A rescue dog, however, may initially have a high escape-drive, and a puppy should always be supervised outdoors as he may be busy tunneling his way out, or getting into all sorts of other mischief such as only puppies manage to find.

If you are adopting a dog from a shelter, you will almost always have a home check. This can be an advantage, as your outdoor space will be checked over in advance by an experienced eye, in case you have missed any escape routes or hazardous objects. These can then be attended to before you bring your rescue dog home. Even if you are buying a puppy for the first time, it can be worth asking an experienced dog-owning friend to check your yard, and if you don't want to share your pool with your dog, now is the time to fence it off! Further advice in preparing your home and yard may be found in Chapter 4.

Outside of his own back yard, your English Springer Spaniel will also enjoy his regular walks in his special places that he knows well. In your Springer's brain, he has a map made up of all the scents he encounters on these regular walks, and nothing satisfies him more than his daily patrols to check everything is where he left it, and if anything new has occurred since yesterday, it is thoroughly checked out! You may find your Springer is more controllable on his regular circuit, but of course he will always love to discover new places; just be prepared to manage his unbridled excitement!

Many English Springer Spaniels are kept perfectly successfully in towns, with regular walks in local parks, but if you live in an urban area it is important to make trips out to the countryside at weekends and vacations, because the Springer Spaniel was bred as a country dog and his instincts are only fully satisfied in a more rural environment. Water-loving English Springer Spaniels especially love to run through the waves and swim in the ocean, lakes, or rivers. It is especially important, however, to keep your attention on your dog in open countryside, because Springer Spaniels can become blinded by excitement. Be aware of such hazards as strong ocean currents and fast flowing rivers, as even though Springer Spaniels love to swim, they are not strong enough to outswim a rip tide or waterfall. Springer Spaniels are especially prone to accidents where they have set out in pursuit of a scent, so you should use a leash near cliff edges and roads. Your dog should also be microchipped with your up-to-date contact details, and wear a collar with an identity tag in case he should stray.

# Costs of Keeping an English Springer Spaniel

The English Springer Spaniel is a pedigree breed, so the first cost you will encounter is the price tag of the dog, and this will be quite high. On average you may expect to pay $700-$1,000 for an English Springer Spaniel with documented bloodlines. If you are offered a dog at a lower price, you should be suspicious. A puppy that has been produced by indiscriminate and unregistered breeding may turn out to have more health issues further down the road, which will be more expensive in the long run. Buying from unregistered sources also encourages the breeding of puppies born to suffer, so it is a welfare issue for the dog, as well as causing a lot of stress and heartbreak for the owner. If on the other hand, you are adopting a rescue dog from a shelter, you will still need to pay a rehoming fee, which may be in the region of $200-$500. This not only protects the dog by ensuring that it is being adopted for genuine reasons, but also goes partway to cover costs such as neutering, vaccinations, microchipping, fostering, accommodation, feeding, transport, and administration.

The cost of keeping an English Springer Spaniel is generally rated as average. With any dog, there will be the usual outlay in terms of accessories, feeding, vaccinating, and neutering, but if you have selected a well-bred puppy, he should stay healthy well into his senior years. On the other hand, as an active dog, the Springer Spaniel has a higher than average chance of injury. Therefore, insurance for veterinary fees is recommended from the outset, since operations can run into thousands of dollars. Also, once a dog has been treated by a vet for any condition, it will generally be excluded for life, and the cost of maintaining an uninsured dog with a lifelong health condition can become a huge financial burden. Alternatively, some owners prefer to self-insure, where they put aside a regular amount for unforeseen veterinary costs. This can take a lot of self-discipline, and may pay off if the dog remains healthy throughout its life. However in the case where a dog requires an expensive procedure that has no guarantee of success, being able to call on an insurance policy can mean the dog is given a chance, whereas otherwise there might be no other choice than euthanasia.

You will also have other regular healthcare costs such as parasite treatments and annual vaccinations which should figure in the budget.

When it comes to feeding your English Springer Spaniel, he is a medium-sized dog with an average appetite, and his feed costs are therefore average. However, he is an active dog and his joints will take a pounding over the course of his lifetime, so to protect them, you will want to be sure he is on a high quality diet, possibly with some supplementation. Nutrition is discussed in Chapter 11. If you wish to work out the likely cost of feeding an adult Springer Spaniel in order to budget for this expenditure, you firstly need to identify which type of food you want for your dog. You can then check on the package or the manufacturer's website for the recommended quantities for an adult weight Springer (40-50 pounds). Calculate the number of portions in the sack, the number of cans per day, or the volume of raw meat if this is your preference, and you will then have a good idea of the cost of feeding your dog month by month. Of course, every dog needs

*Photo Courtesy of Andrew MacVicar*

the occasional treat, whether it is a daily dental chew, a pig's ear, antler, or the training treats you will need in the early stages, so you should add these into the budget too.

Chapter 4 gives an idea of the basic equipment you will need for your Springer Spaniel. Some of these items may well last a lifetime, but others will be outgrown, worn out, or destroyed over the course of time, and will need replacing. For many owners, shopping for their dogs gives them a lot of pleasure, whereas others may need to keep expenses to a minimum and look out for bargains and secondhand items. Either way, your dog doesn't mind how much has been spent on him as long as his equipment is safe and clean.

There are many optional extras when it comes to the cost of keeping an English Springer Spaniel, and a lot of these depend upon which activities you wish to participate in with your dog. Initially, there is the training stage. This does not have to cost anything at all if you feel confident to train your dog from previous experience, or in consultation with books or the internet. However, your puppy will benefit from socialization in a class setting where he can meet lots of dogs of a wide variety of breeds, but all at the same life stage. These classes often charge a nominal fee, as will the formal training classes that follow. However, this is a great investment for your dog's future.

If you plan to show your dog, you can begin when your puppy is six months. There is no doubt showing is an expensive hobby, but one that brings a lot of pleasure and pride to many owners. You will need to keep your dog in prime physical and cosmetic condition, and as well as grooming expenses you will have to cover show fees and travel costs. Owners who have purchased a Springer Spaniel from working lines may have intentions to hunt, and this will incur costs such as equipment, training, and permits. Other owners might like the idea of participating in Agility and Flyball, which will always involve a class fee, and competition fees if your dog progresses.

Generally, the expenses involved in keeping an English Springer Spaniel are not excessive, and a good many of them are optional. Therefore, you can keep the costs to a level that suits you, and budget carefully for the future. So ownership of an English Springer Spaniel does not have to preclude those on lower incomes. All that matters to your English Springer Spaniel is that he is comfortable, cared for, and has human companionship. If you can promise him these basic requirements then he has all he needs. Because the simple fact is, all your Springer Spaniel needs is you.

# CHAPTER 2
# Breed History

## Origin of the Breed

Although the name "Springer Spaniel" was only officially adopted in 1902 by the Sporting Society of Britain and recognized by the English Kennel Club, Spaniels are one of the most historic breeds in Europe. The word Spaniel in itself hints at the presumed origin of the breed, which is thought to have come from Hispania, a Roman province on the Iberian Peninsula, and was brought to Britain by the Romans. Documentary evidence for the existence of Spaniels in Britain exists in an ancient law of Wales dating from 300 AD.

By medieval times, the Spaniel was known to have found its vocation as a hunting dog. At this point in history, firearms were not yet invented, and hunting took place with hawks and dogs, with both birds and mammals being hunted. The Spaniel would flush out the game for hawks, coursing hounds or nets. The physical appearance of the hunting Spaniel from this time would not have been dissimilar to the English Springer Spaniel we

recognize today, as evidenced by paintings and prints from the 16th and 17th centuries. In 1576, Johannes Caius described the Land Spaniel as, *"Nearly all white. If they have any spots, these are red, and scarce and big. There is also a red and black variety."* And in 1637, Italian naturalist Aldrovandrus wrote of the Land Spaniel that it possessed, *"Floppy ears, the chest, belly, and feet, white, picked (ticked) out with black, the rest of the body black."*

In the 17th century, the wheel lock firearm was invented, and flying shooting became possible, so the Spaniel would spring the game for the gun rather than a hawk, dog, or net.

## HISTORY LESSON
### Mayflower Dogs

In 1620, two dogs owned by John Goodman came to Cape Cod aboard the *Mayflower*. Though the names of these dogs have been lost to history, it is believed that one of them was a Spaniel. The Spaniel's role in the early colony was likely hunting game birds. It's impossible to say whether or not this Spaniel was a true English Springer because the *Mayflower* voyage took place 253 years before the foundation of the Kennel Club in England, and 282 years before the English Springer Spaniel breed was recognized by the aforementioned club in 1902.

From this time onward, the Springer Spaniel's role has remained very little changed over the centuries. Even the dog's character remains as true today as it was then, as described by 17th century sportsman, Richard Surflet:

*"The spaniel is gentle, loving and courteous to man more than any other dog, of free untiring laborsome ranging, beating a full course over and over, which he does with a wanton playing taile and a busie labouring noise, neither desisting nor showing less delight in his labours at night than he did in the morning."*

## Genetics

Up until the 20th century, there would have been no genetic difference between the Springer and the Cocker Spaniel, as they would come from the same litter, the only differentiation being that the smaller dogs were selected to hunt woodcock, and the larger littermates were used to spring game. In the 18th century, the Duke of Norfolk allegedly began breeding hunting spaniels, and called them Norfolk Spaniels, although the precise attribution of the breed is still a subject for controversy as later Dukes of Norfolk denied any involvement. The breed was generally known as the Land Spaniel to differentiate it from the Water Spaniel, although the English Water Span-

Photo Courtesy of
Demelza Slaney

iel was certainly a genetic contributor to the mix. The Land Spaniel was divided into the Crouching Spaniel and the Springing Spaniel. The Springing Spaniel was later subdivided by size, when in 1801, the natural history illustrator Sydenham Teast Edwards suggested in his encyclopedia of British dog breeds, Cynographia Britannica, that an official distinction should be recognized between the Springing, Hawking Spaniel, or Starter, and the Cocking, or Cocker Spaniel.

In the 19th century, dogs weighing up to 25 lbs were called Cockers or Cocking Spaniels, and the larger dogs were known as Field Spaniels or English Spaniels. A purpose-bred genetic distinction only began to be introduced when a strain of English Springer Spaniels known as Shropshire Spaniels, was started by the Boughey family of Aqualate in Shopshire. Mop 1, whelped in 1812, was its first representative. The Boughey strain was kept in the family for over a century, producing the champion F.T.Ch. Velox Powder in 1903. The previous year, the English Kennel Club first recognized the breed and the Norfolk and Shropshire Spaniels became absorbed under the English Springer Spaniel umbrella. For a decade, English Springer Spaniels gained recognition in the show ring, and in 1913, the first English Springer Spaniel with a documented pedigree arrived in Canada from Britain, beginning the emergence of the breed in North America. The First World War put a stop to showing in the UK, only to be revived in the 1920s, with the founding of the English Springer Spaniel Club in 1921. From this point, the famous kennel names emerged, such as Tissington, Avendale, Beechgrove, Horsford, Velox, Denne, Laverstoke, and Rivington.

# Divergence within the Breed

*"Springers were initially bred to hunt! However, for the last 60 years the breed has basically split into two different types of dogs. The 'Field bred' and the 'Show bred'. Figure out which dog is going to suit your specific needs/desires."*

**Randy Huffey**
*Huffey's Springers*

During the inter-war years, there was no distinction between show breeds and working breeds, and many dogs would go straight from the show ring to the field the next day, and vice versa. Field trials and conformation were of equal importance to the early breeders in the United States. Dogs that excelled equally in both these disciplines were known as "dual-type" or "dual-purpose" Springer Spaniels; however, the last dual championship was earned in the early 1940s, after which the breed began to diverge as field trial enthusiasts selected for working qualities, and breeders who favored the show ring sought to conform closely to the official breed standard.

Careful specialization since this time has resulted in a distinction in appearance and temperament between the working Springer and its show-bred counterpart. The working Springer Spaniel is a high energy athlete with a shorter, lighter coat, whereas the show Springer, also known as the bench type, will display evenness of temperament and physique, and a long coat with impressive feathering. This important distinction is often overlooked by the novice owner and will be discussed further in Chapter 5, *"How to Choose an English Springer Spaniel."*

# Famous English Springer Spaniels in History

Probably the earliest celebrity Spaniel of Springer type was owned by Scottish independence fighter William "Braveheart" Wallace in the late 13th century. Wallace's Spaniel was named Merlin and he rode into the Battle of Sterling Bridge alongside his master in 1297. Although this was many centuries before the English Springer Spaniel was recognized, and Wallace of course was staunchly Scottish, Merlin was an early representative ancestor of the breed.

We have mentioned the first official English Springer Spaniel arrived in North America in 1913, but one of the 102 passengers who sailed to the New World aboard the Mayflower in 1620 was John Goodman. Naturally he could not leave his dogs behind, one of which was a Springer-type Spaniel whose name is not known. Although Goodman died soon after arrival in America, his dogs were cared for by the Pilgrims, and his Spaniel is immortalized in a painting by Leon Gerome Ferris, entitled, *The First Thanksgiving, 1621.*

American Presidents always require a First Dog, and this office was once held by Millie, owned by George H.W. Bush, and Spot, owned by his son George W. Bush. Millie, a brown and white Springer, was named after a family friend, Mildred Caldwell Kerr. She was referred to as the most famous dog in White House history, after her master stated during his 1992 reelection speech, "My dog Millie knows more about foreign affairs than these two bozos." As well as foreign affairs, Millie also had a vocation in TV, appearing in *Murphy Brown, Wings,* and *Who's the Boss,* as well as *The Simpsons.*

One of Millie's puppies became George W. Bush's dog, Spot Fetcher, poetically named after baseball player Scott Fletcher. She was also brown and white, and was the first dog to live in the White House during two consecutive terms of office.

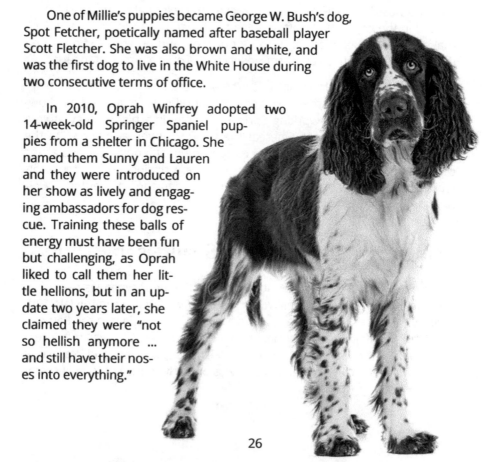

In 2010, Oprah Winfrey adopted two 14-week-old Springer Spaniel puppies from a shelter in Chicago. She named them Sunny and Lauren and they were introduced on her show as lively and engaging ambassadors for dog rescue. Training these balls of energy must have been fun but challenging, as Oprah liked to call them her little hellions, but in an update two years later, she claimed they were "not so hellish anymore ... and still have their noses into everything."

# Springer Spaniel Variants, Hybrids, and Crossbreeds

In more recent history, the popularity of the English Springer Spaniel has soared; however, new owners are now searching for variants and cross-breeds, to ensure they have all the good English Springer Spaniel traits, mixed with the desirable traits of others.

## Welsh Springer Spaniel

*Welsh Springer Spaniel*

The Welsh Springer Spaniel is not a derivative of the English Springer Spaniel, but an independent breed in its own right, with bloodlines going back to the same early Land Spaniel ancestors as its English cousin. To look at, the Welsh Springer Spaniel is similar to the English Springer Spaniel, with its dual color feathered coat and long curly ears, but it is smaller in size, and always red-brown and white, the color being more red than the English Springer Spaniel's brown, or "liver," variant. The Welsh Springer Spaniel is full of energy and enthusiasm, requiring a lot of daily exercise, but excels both in the field and as a pet, being good with children and other pets.

The Welsh Springer Spaniel gained recognition by the British Kennel Club in 1902, at the same time as the English Springer Spaniel; however, the First World War disrupted the registered breeding program with the result that it had to be restarted with unregistered dogs in the 1920s. In the USA, no Welsh Springer Spaniels were thought to remain after the Second World War, with the result that all dogs of this breed today in the US and Canada are descendants of those reintroduced in the 1940s. In the UK and across the world, the Welsh Springer Spaniel remains relatively few in number, and in 2016 the British Kennel Club included it on their list of vulnerable native breeds.

## Sprocker Spaniel

*Sprocker Spaniel*

The Sprocker is one of the most well-known and popular modern hybrid breeds. As the name suggests, the Sprocker came about through crossing the English Springer Spaniel with the Cocker Spaniel. The fact that both parents are Spaniels mean that this is not a crossbreed. In many ways it is a reversion to the earlier ancestry of the breeds, since Springer and Cocker Spaniels originally came from the same litter.

Sprockers were developed to produce a tough and reliable gundog breed, so the favored combination is for both parents to be working types, with a Cocker Spaniel Sire and a Springer Spaniel dam. Stockier puppies are produced if the Cocker sire is a show type. Recently, Sprockers are now being produced from parents who are both Sprockers themselves. However, the breed has not yet been officially recognized by the British Kennel Club.

The typical Sprocker is the size of a small Springer Spaniel and of similar appearance, but they often take their coloration from the Cocker, being mostly seen with solid black or chocolate coat colors. There is more variety in the coat color of the Sprocker than in either parent, as they may be solid, roan, piebald liver, black and white, tricolor, or mostly solid with white markings.

Sprockers inherit the temperament of their Springer and Cocker Spaniel parents, along with the high energy of the working Springer breed. As they are very popular but not yet recognized by the Kennel Club, breeding can be unregulated, so the purchaser should be careful in selecting a puppy, taking the advice given in Chapter 5.

## Springerdoodle/Sprockerdoodle

One of the most popular trends in recent years is the crossing of pure breeds with the poodle, to create (in theory) a dog with a non-shedding coat. This can vary in the result, with some dogs inheriting more of the woolly, low-shedding poodle coat, and others inheriting a silkier coat from their Springer Spaniel parent which will shed more and require more grooming.

The poodle is also favored for hybrid breeding because of its temperament, producing a good-natured, friendly, and entertaining dog that slots in well as part of the family.

The Springerdoodle or Sprockerdoodle is not recognized by the Kennel Club in Britain or America as it is a designer breed, but it is recognized by various international designer breed registries.

## Springador

The Springador is a crossbreed from the Springer Spaniel and the Labrador. Although its origins are unclear, the fact that these two breeds live and work together in the hunting field makes the pairing a compatible one with many favorable characteristics, especially in temperament, as both breeds are exceptionally biddable and loyal, with the more placid Labrador toning down the unbridled excitability of the Springer Spaniel.

Springadors can vary greatly in appearance as the parent breeds are quite different. So coat length, feathering, and head shape can vary, as can the wide range of coloration, which may be yellow, golden, brown, chocolate, or black, with or without white markings.

Although they originate from working breeds, Springadors make excellent pets, being playful and sociable, and are more chilled than their Spaniel parent. They do, however, require a high level of exercise and mental stimulation.

As the Springador is not a recognized Kennel Club breed and breeding is therefore unregulated, purchasers should be careful in selecting their puppy, following the advice in Chapter 5.

*Springador*

## Spangold Retriever

*Photo Courtesy of
Heiley @heileythespangold on Instagram*

The Spangold Retriever is a similar cross to the Springador, but the parent breed is the Golden Retriever rather than the Labrador. The Golden Retriever is also found working in the field, like the Labrador and the Springer Spaniel, but the difference is its luxuriant shedding coat. Coupled with the luscious locks of the English Springer Spaniel, it is clear that the offspring of this designer combination will look stunning, but shed copiously.

Counterintuitively, the Spangold Retriever does not commonly have a golden coat, but is usually black with white markings on his chest and paws. He may also have gold or russet markings. The

*Spangold Retriever*

Spangold Retriever is more sedentary than the English Springer Spaniel, but is also larger, and requires plenty of exercise to stay in good shape.

## Sprollie/Border Springer

*Sprollie-Border Springer*

The Border Collie is an intensely high energy, hugely intelligent working dog used for herding sheep and cattle. If the English Springer Spaniel is not energetic and intense enough, then crossing the breed with a Border Collie will be sure to produce a dynamic ball of energy with the sort of stamina and enthusiasm to take on any physical or mental challenge thrown at it.

This particular crossbreed would have originated naturally on farms in the past, and would produce an effective working dog. But with the emergence of designer breeds, anyone taking on a Sprollie as a pet should be sure of their commitment to meeting the exercise and intellectual stimulation needs of the breed. Agility and flyball are activities very suited to the domestic Sprollie.

As with any crossbreed that is not regulated by the Kennel Club, purchasers should be careful in choosing a puppy, ensuring the parents are free of any genetic diseases common to either of the parent breeds.

## Spreagle/Beagle Springer

The Beagle and the Springer Spaniel may seem like very different dogs, but both have hunting in their genes, and are similarly proportioned, so the mix can produce a good-looking dog with an instinct to hunt and retrieve, and boundless energy.

The Beagle Springer is not a breed for the novice owner, as its instincts will be very much to the fore and will need to be channeled into a working life or certainly a very active domestic life. Early training with this cross breed is particularly important, especially recall.

## Dalmatian Spaniel

The Dalmatian Spaniel is another cross breed that is sure to have arisen from accidental breeding in earlier times, but with the current trend for designer breeds, is now being produced more purposefully.

Dalmatian Spaniels may be a mix of the Dalmatian with the English Springer or the Cocker Spaniel, so there will be some variety in the resulting offspring. Also, as with all early generation crossbreeds, where the parents are of two distinct breeds, rather than

*Dalmatian Spaniel*

both of the same crossbreed, the puppies may take on the predominant traits and appearance of either parent, so his coat may be short or longer, with spots or flecks and patches. It will usually be black and white with the occasional appearance of liver brown coloration if either parent has this in the mix.

The Dalmatian Spaniel is sure to have a good temperament as both breeds are intelligent, trainable, and eager to please. Some dogs, however, can inherit the aloofness and the guarding instincts of the Dalmatian so early socialization is essential, along with plenty of exercise to guard against a predisposition to obesity.

It is clear that the English Springer Spaniel, having been distilled down the centuries from a very generic breed, now appears in many guises, being crossed with other distinct breeds. The important factor to remember in choosing a designer breed is that not all of these mixes will be successful, and the arbitrary nature of early-generation crosses means that the puppies may inherit the worst qualities of each parent breed rather than the best. They may also be unsuitable as domestic pets, so the onus is on the

owner to do their homework into the mix of breeds. Also, the owner is far more on their own in the selection of a healthy puppy, as while these cross breeds are not recognized by the Kennel Clubs across the world, breeding is unregulated, and parents may be indiscriminately selected, and not routinely tested for genetic conditions.

Whether you choose a pure red English Springer Spaniel or a dog with Springer Spaniel in its genetics, the advice given in Chapter 5 in selecting a dog is relevant. And an understanding of the English Springer Spaniel, as set out in this book, will help you appreciate the character and needs of the breed.

*Photo Courtesy of
Trevor Kerr
www.trevkerrphotographer.com*

# CHAPTER 3
# Behavior

## Temperament

The English Springer Spaniel is one of the UK's most popular dogs, and known throughout the world. With an exceptionally long heritage, and an adaptability that means Springers can be found both in the field and in the family home, the breed seems naturally familiar and it's easy to feel that you know what to expect from a Springer Spaniel: friendliness, intelligence, loyalty, goofiness, and fun. It is true these qualities abound in the breed; however, there is so much more to consider in the English Springer Spaniel, especially if you are considering sharing your life with this beautiful but complex dog.

Chapter 2 discussed the development of the English Springer Spaniel breed over a period of 1,000 years, and for many centuries there was little change in the Springer Spaniel's ancestors from one generation to the next, being bred for hunting and given a job based upon sorting the littermates by size. It is only comparatively recently that selective breeding has produced the English Springer Spaniel as a recognized breed, and more recently still that a divergence has emerged between the working and the show (or bench) versions of the breed. This distinction is important in understanding the temperament of the English Springer Spaniel and managing his behavior.

> ## FUN FACT 😊
> ### Award-Winning Springers
>
> Between 1924 and 2019, fifteen English Springer Spaniels have been named sporting group winners at the Westminster Dog Show. The most recent English Springer Spaniel to win in this category was GCH. Wynmoor Sweetgrass White Diamonds, owned by Dr. Erin Kerfoot, Billie Kerfoot, and Dr. Alison Smith, in 2015.

The Springer Spaniel is still most widely recognized as a working dog, but a breed that is also happy in a family home. However, this easy adaptability can be its downfall if the domestic owner takes on a dog from working stock rather than show lines without realizing the distinction. On the other hand, the owner who intends to hunt with his Springer Spaniel will be purposely seeking out the qualities of a working dog that make him more challenging as a domestic pet, these being a high prey drive, bravery, intensity, relentless inexhaustible energy, and an independent spirit.

In contrast, the show-bred English Springer Spaniel, while still full of personality and intelligence, is a slightly quieter, gentler dog, more inclined to form close human attachments, though sometimes to the point of emotional neediness. Expecting a show-bred English Springer Spaniel to excel as a gundog could be a recipe for disaster, as a gunshot may leave this sensitive dog quivering and confused. He will also be more at home with his human family than housed in gundog kennels with his canine companions.

It should be noted that a rare genetic condition can occur in show-bred Springer Spaniels, called rage syndrome, or idiopathic aggression. This is a sudden-onset aggressive outburst that is completely out of character, and may be accompanied by a glazed or absent appearance. This neurological condition is different from what Spaniel owners like to refer to as "red mist," when their dog is gripped by the excitement of its prey drive in the field and completely unresponsive to recall.

With these two distinct groupings within the breed, it can be seen that making generalizations about the temperament of the English Springer Spaniel is hard to do. However, even between two working dogs or two show dogs, differences will be apparent, as any seasoned owner of Springer Spaniels will tell you, and no two dogs are the same. They are all full of character, but each dog has their own distinct personality. This is all part of the fun of bringing an English Springer Spaniel into your life. There is only one thing that can be guaranteed, and that is that there will never be a dull moment!

So what is it exactly about the temperament of the Springer Spaniel that makes him an international favorite? To begin with, this is an exceptionally intelligent dog, and with intelligence comes the ability to communicate, especially as the Springer Spaniel has an empathetic connection with humans, making him affectionate, loyal, and eager to please. As long as the Springer Spaniel's natural intelligence is harnessed by training him from an early age, a bond will develop between dog and owner that forms the basis of an unshakeable relationship. This is true of both the working and show strains, and marks the breed out as one that in many ways seems almost human. A connection this strong is the reason the English Springer Spaniel holds such a high place in human affection.

# Trainability

*"ESS are really smart dogs that are easily trained with the use of positive reinforcement. Just don't forget, they are puppies! Consistency and patience is needed."*

**Dawn Horock**
*Daz-End English Springer Spaniels*

As a breed that originally developed as a working dog, the English Springer Spaniel has always been highly trainable, and this quality still exists in both the working and show lines. It is, however, vitally important to harness this trainability from a very young age so that your dog, whether working in the field or adapting to family life, is looking to his owner for all his cues, and not using his innate intelligence to make up his own rules. With the working strain, the owner has the added challenge of channeling the dog's heightened animal instincts into the makings of a highly effective gundog. So working Springers in particular need to be guided by expe-

Photo Courtesy of Carol Farmer

rienced owners; it is an unfortunate statistic that more working Springers than show-bred Springers end up in rescue by owners who were not prepared for the high level of training required. Having said that, no English Springer Spaniel will train itself, and it always requires the commitment of the owner from the outset to shape the dog into the best version of itself.

Your approach to training will depend to some extent on whether you are taking on a show-bred puppy, a working-bred puppy, or an adult dog from a rescue or previous home. Springer Spaniels are naturally friendly toward both humans and other dogs, and the earliest training you can do with your puppy is socialization, which will be discussed further in Chapter 8. In some cases, however, a rogue working strain may produce a less sociable dog, or a dog from a rescue may have experienced cruelty in the past, making him wary, or even aggressive to strangers. It is not the usual experience

Photo Courtesy of Emma Coxon

of a Springer Spaniel owner to have to work to gain the dog's trust since the breed is naturally so human-friendly, but where the dog may have been failed by bad breeding or mankind's mistreatment, it can be left to the new owner to rehabilitate the dog psychologically for the best chance of a happy life alongside its human companion.

The English Springer Spaniel is a particularly sensitive dog, and training should always be positive and reward-based, building trust between dog and owner. Harsh training methods, while generally no longer in favor, should definitely be avoided in the case of the Springer Spaniel.

Assuming your English Springer Spaniel has been socialized, and has learned basic commands such as those in Chapter 9, and recall as discussed in Chapter 7, then further training may diverge according to what you wish to do with your dog. Those who intend to hunt with their dog will be looking at advanced gundog training, discussed in Chapter 16, whereas those who are just looking for a fun and active family pet may not feel the need for further training other than consolidation of the basic commands. However, it should be recognized that during the dog's adolescence, from about 9 months, a previously well-trained and obedient Springer Spaniel may appear to regress. This is a natural stage and the owner should not feel discouraged, but continue to reinforce reward-based training, with extra vigilance in situations where the dog might run into danger through ignoring a previously good recall.

# Exercise Requirements

English Springer Spaniels are a high-energy dog and require at least two hours of exercise a day. This is not only important for their physical health and weight control, but also for their mental well-being, as they are always very enthusiastic for the outdoors. This is because overnight tracks left by small animals provide a stimulus to their keen sense of smell that absolutely have to be investigated, and there is nothing that can compare with a bush full of sticky burrs or a muddy puddle. Springer Spaniels will always find water if there is any to be found. They will also benefit from swimming in the sea or safe inland lakes and waterways, which is an excellent form of exercise. However, the owner should be mindful of currents, stagnant water, and toxic blue-green algae, as well as respecting wildfowl and fishermen, who require their space to be undisturbed.

In order for a Springer Spaniel to meet its exercise requirement, it needs to be exercised off the lead because the ground coverage of the dog in two hours will vastly outstrip the capabilities of even the fittest owner. So good recall is essential, and this is discussed in Chapter 7. Ball games can also pack a lot of physical exercise into a shorter time frame. Springer Spaniels love to play ball and have a talent for retrieval and searching out lost balls. However, hard exercise of this nature is not recommended for young dogs owing to their developing growth plates, and older dogs may hurt their backs with the hard turns involved. Plus relentless ball games deprive the dog of exercising its animal instincts, so balance and moderation is the key to getting the most out of your dog's exercise time.

Working Springer Spaniels will be getting their daily exercise requirement and mental stimulation out in the field, but domestic Springers may benefit from extra physical activities, such as Canicross (running with your dog), Agility, and Flyball. These activities are listed in descending order of physical demands on the owner. Advanced physical activities such as these may only be started once your dog is fully grown, to protect his developing bones, but Springer Spaniels may excel at and enjoy these challenges. However, some Springer Spaniels are especially sensitive, and may find these activities stressful, especially Agility with its intimidating obstacles. So, the owner should be mindful of their own dog, and look for exercise opportunities that he enjoys and that help his brain to unwind rather than the opposite.

# Hyperactivity

If your dog is getting at least two hours of exercise a day, and he is still hyperactive, there may be some reasons and coping strategies you can consider.

Quite often, owners of hyperactive Springer Spaniels have inadvertently purchased a domestic pet from working stock, and as we have already discussed, there is a marked distinction between how the working lines are bred, so the energy and stamina of a working dog will never be exhausted, which can be very draining. So often, the owner will realize their mistake, give up on the dog, and place it in rescue, or try to find it a working home. Unfortunately, if the dog is no longer a young puppy, vital training months will have been missed, and the dog will have become a problem dog that even an experienced huntsman may not wish to take on. For this reason, it cannot be stressed enough that owners looking for a pet should select from show lines, not working lines, as it is failing the dog if his exercise needs can never be met from the outset.

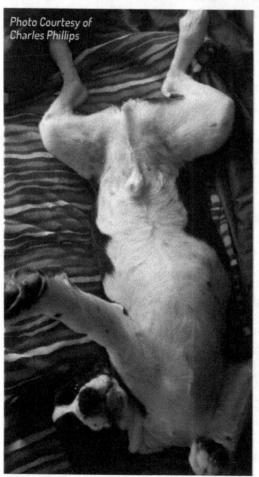

Photo Courtesy of Charles Phillips

If however, you do have a high-energy dog in the home, whatever its breeding, additional ways to address the issue may involve Canicross, Agility, or Flyball, as previously mentioned, or the additional services of a dog walker. Some trainers also recommend a backpack to give the dog extra weight to carry when on a walk, army-style.

Your hyperactive dog's busy mind will rarely be at

rest in the home, so in order to prevent destructive behavior, you need to give him something to occupy himself, such as a stuffed Kong® or a raw bone (never a cooked bone which may splinter), or preferably a deer antler. You should also look at his diet and discuss with your veterinarian or a canine dietician whether his food has excess sugars or additives, and whether another food would be better suited to him. Your vet will also be able to test for any underlying conditions that may be contributing to your dog's hyperactivity.

You should also look at yourself as an owner, as the Springer Spaniel is an especially sensitive dog and will pick up on any anxiety and stress in the home. Try to keep a calm and structured environment in place for him with a regular routine, and your dog will begin to recognize periods for downtime, which will benefit him just as much as his owner. Dogs that have been crate-trained from a puppy actually find their crate a safe place where they can retreat and relax, so crate training from the outset can preempt the difficulties of a hyperactive dog further down the line.

This chapter has provided an overview of the types of behaviors you might expect from your English Springer Spaniel. It should only be considered a guide, as whereas the breed is founded on a happy, playful, loving, and loyal temperament, Springer Spaniels are so full of their own personalities that you never get to know your dog until he shares his life with you. One thing is for certain, though, in training your dog, he will also be training you to become physically fitter, more patient, more understanding, a more consistent disciplinarian, more capable of love, and to take life a lot less seriously. In giving up a part of your life to share it with a Springer Spaniel, yours will be enriched in turn, and every day will be brighter and full of fun.

# CHAPTER 4
# Preparations for a New Dog

If you have owned dogs before, or if you already have a resident dog, then you are already aware of the things you need to consider before bringing a new dog into the home. For new dog owners, preparing to welcome the new arrival can seem both exciting and daunting. The list of things to buy seems endless, and naturally you want the dog to fit in and make himself at home from day one. This chapter will help you to focus on the essentials, and for those who already have had a dog now or in the past, it will still help to know a few specifics relating to Springer Spaniels.

# Preparing Your Home

*"I'd suggest they prepare their new home just like they would if they had a toddler in the house. Have everything out of reach you do not want the puppy to get. Have a crate in the house. The rule of thumb, of course, is that a puppy is either in the crate or watched 100% of the time while out of the crate. If you take your eye off the puppy, it will ether destroy something or have an accident in the house. They learn quickly, but they are puppies!"*

**Tim Whitney**
*ESS Breeder*

If you have reserved a puppy, you probably have a few weeks to prepare your home before your lovable ball of dynamite arrives, and nothing will be quite the same again! Those who have ever lost a dog will say how empty their home feels without one, so in a few short weeks, your home and your life will be full, and when you are welcoming a Springer Spaniel, you can guarantee that full means to the maximum!

If you are adopting a Springer Spaniel from a rescue, part of the process will involve a home check. This may sound intimidating, but the representative from the rescue center is not looking for dust above the door frames, but merely making sure that you live where you say you do, that if you rent then your rental agreement permits you to keep a dog, that all the family are in agreement about keeping a dog, and that your home is safe for the dog. If you have not had a dog before, the experienced home checker may make suggestions for certain things that need to be attended to before the dog arrives. You are not likely to fail a home check because you have overlooked something as long as you are willing to fix it, although the home checker may come back before the dog arrives to ensure, for instance, that the broken fence panel they noticed has been replaced.

If you are buying a puppy, it is unlikely that you will be home checked, although some breeders may wish to see where their puppy is going. This means that if you have not had a dog before,

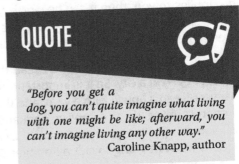

**QUOTE**

*"Before you get a dog, you can't quite imagine what living with one might be like; afterward, you can't imagine living any other way."*
Caroline Knapp, author

Photo Courtesy of
Carol Farmer

you will not have an experienced eye to make sure everything is in place. If this applies to you, then it can be worth asking a friend with experience of similar sized dogs to check over your house and garden. Most would be flattered to be asked, and to share in the excitement of the impending arrival.

The Springer Spaniel is not a breed that is suited to living in an apartment, or even in a city. So it is important before even considering the breed that you live in a house with a yard, and that you live within driving distance of open countryside or extensive parkland for the two hours of daily exercise your dog will require as an adult. Living outside in the yard, however large, is also not going to suit a Springer Spaniel, as he craves companionship. Even working Springers that live in kennels have the companionship of their canine friends and the attention of their handler for much of the day. A domestic Springer Spaniel needs human company, and it is a characteristic of the Springer Spaniel that he bonds closely with one particular person, his primary caregiver and trainer. He will only be happy living in the house with that person, in as close proximity as he is allowed.

Deciding on that proximity is a consideration you should make before your dog even arrives. Some owners may be happy for their dog to have the run of the house, and to have their dog sleep on the upstairs landing, in the bedroom, or even on the bed once it is housebroken. Others may wish to confine the dog to the rooms downstairs, or even certain rooms, so that others can be kept dog-free. When you have decided where your dog will be allowed, you may section off certain doorways or the stairs with stair gates. Otherwise, keeping doors shut to the dog-free rooms may suffice. You may also wish to consider sectioning off your hallway near the front door to prevent your dog rushing out until he is fully trained.

The decision whether to allow your dog in the bedrooms or on the bed is not simply a matter of whether it would be nice for the dog or for yourself. If you have children, it may be advisable to train your dog to sleep downstairs, or to ban the dog from the bedrooms if you live in a single-story house. This is because by having access to the adult bedroom or by sleeping with the adults of the household, the dog may develop a sense of superiority over the children, which may result in aggression, snarling, or snapping. This is discussed further in Chapter 8.

Whether or not you intend to crate train your dog, a crate can still be useful for the dog to use voluntarily as a safe space, so you should think about where to position it. This will usually be where you expect your dog to sleep at night, but he will be happiest to use it if it is where he can see you during the evening. If you have a large house, you may need multiple crates, so your dog can be near you while you prepare food, eat, or watch television, as Springer Spaniels are particularly inclined to follow their owner around the house at all times. The crate should be out of drafts and strong sunlight, and if it does not have a cover, you can use blankets or towels to cover the crate at night to signal to the dog that it is time to settle.

Think about where you wish to feed your dog. This will usually be the kitchen or utility room, but should be on a hard floor where water and spilled food can easily be cleaned up. You should also think about where you will store your dog's food, especially if you are feeding dry kibble. This should be kept in an inaccessible place such as a cupboard, storage container, or on a high shelf, as ingesting a large amount of stolen kibble could be serious for your dog.

Now is also the time to put away any objects that you do not wish your dog to destroy, as puppies will chew indiscriminately, especially while they are teething. If you have children, you should encourage them to keep their toys tidied away if they are in rooms to which the dog will have access. Also if you have any expensive furniture, you may wish to remove it while your new dog is at the puppy stage.

It is important for an active dog such as a Springer Spaniel to have access to your yard to exercise, play, and relieve himself. The yard needs to be fully secure, as your new dog will usually not be trained and will not necessarily respect the boundaries of your house in the early stages. A six-foot-high perimeter fence is recommended for an athletic dog such as a Springer Spaniel. The fence should also come fully to the ground, and a watchful eye should be kept on the dog until it is known whether or not he is a tunneler, as some dogs will dig under a fence if left unsupervised.

You should fit a lock to your back gate to deter opportunist thieves, as a Springer Spaniel is a pedigree dog and high on the list of desirable breeds for dog thieves.

Bear in mind that your dog will be using your yard for his toileting habits, so you should have a scoop ready to deal with the daily mess, and if you have children, you may wish to section your yard to keep a part of it reliably mess-free. Also if you have a pond or swimming pool, your Springer Spaniel will be unable to resist the allure of water, so you may wish to section off these areas too.

If you are a keen gardener, you may have to prepare yourself for the fact that a puppy will take great pleasure in digging up your plants, so if you have any that are particularly special to you, you may wish to replant them elsewhere. Also be aware of any plants in your garden that are toxic to dogs as these should be removed, along with slug pellets, mouse traps, and rat bait. If you have a garden shed, be sure that any chemical hazards are on a high shelf or in a cupboard.

If you already have a dog, you may feel fully prepared for your new arrival, but some considerations may still apply. For example, your resident dog knows where he lives and has no inclination to escape, so maybe your boundary has not been checked recently, and perhaps there is a hole in the fence, or a fox tunnel in the corner. Maybe your fence is only three feet high because your resident dog is a small breed that does not jump. Also, although your resident dog has never shown the remotest interest in the swimming pool, and it will be a while before any new puppy finds his water-wings, if you are adopting an adult Springer Spaniel there is a certain guarantee that he will be doing lengths before he has even said hello.

In the home, if your resident dog already has access to the bedrooms you will not be able to make a separate rule for the new dog, and it would seem unfair and confusing for the resident dog to introduce sudden restrictions. However, the dominant behavior mentioned previously when a dog is allowed to share bedroom space with adult humans will face the added dynamic of another dog. This could go either way. It may distract the newcomer from challenging the children's place in the hierarchy, or the new dog may contest the resident dog for superiority, or the resident dog may be defensive of his position. If dominance issues arise, both dogs may have to accept new sleeping arrangements, and getting the new dog used to a crate from the outset is a good insurance policy against problems further down the line. This is discussed further in Chapter 8.

Also, although your resident dog may not be destructive, a puppy almost certainly will, so it is wise to put away any chewable objects in the short term, and certainly not replace your carpets for a while. A bit of sympathetic foresight at this stage will ensure that your relationship with your new dog gets off on a happy note, without unfair expectations being placed on him, as he finds his paws in his new home.

Photo Courtesy of Jill Martinez

# Shopping List

*"Toys are a must since most English Springer Spaniels love their toys. Try getting some of the new interactive toys to help them to think and learn. There are many of these new toys on the market."*

**Judy Ann Manley**
*Vistah Kennels*

Shopping for a new dog can be both exciting and expensive. Just venturing into the pet store will make you aware of the vast array of pet accessories waiting to make a dent in your wallet. But if you are on a budget, there is no need to spend a fortune on your new arrival at this stage. Just selecting the essentials will ensure that you have all you need to get started, without wasting money on things you may never use or that your dog will outgrow or show no interest in.

Before you pick up your dog, it is worth ordering an identification tag as this may take a few days to be engraved. It is advisable that your new dog should wear an ID tag on his collar from day one with your cell phone number and address, because the early days are when he is most at risk of straying. Adult rescue dogs can be especially prone to absconding, as they may be confused and wish to get back to familiar territory. Or the reason they were in rescue in the first place may be because they strayed and could not be reunited. An identification tag simplifies the process of reuniting a stray dog, especially if the microchip details have not yet been updated. Your dog's ID tag will not usually carry his name, so this is not an issue if you have not yet decided on it.

Your dog will need a collar and lead. The collar should be adjustable for your growing dog. Webbing is a good choice as it is strong and withstands getting wet, although leather collars are a traditional choice for gundogs. If you choose a leather collar be sure to check it regularly around the buckle where it may weaken and break from wear.

Choke chains, otherwise known as check chains, are no longer in favor as a training aid as they can cause damage to the dog, and your sensitive Springer Spaniel in any case responds best to positive reinforcement, not harsh training methods.

You will need a short webbing or leather leash to clip onto your collar. A short leash is used in training classes, and is safer than a flexi-leash when out and about near traffic, as the lock on a flexi-leash may sometimes fail, especially if the dog is pulling. If you choose a flexi-leash, it should only be

Photo Courtesy of
Sophie Gibbs

used away from traffic, people, and other dogs, and is no substitute for re-call training, which will be discussed in Chapter 7.

Although in training classes the leash is usually attached to the collar, a harness is strongly recommended for your dog when out and about. This is because until your dog learns to walk on a loose leash, which can be a challenge for a lively Springer Spaniel, it can damage the neck bones and larynx if the dog pulls on a collar. A harness spreads the tension and diverts it across the chest. This is even more important if your dog runs to the end of the leash causing a sudden jerk, which would hurt the neck if the dog was being led off a collar. A well-fitting harness is also safer, as a dog can back out of a collar, which could be dangerous near traffic. If you are preparing for a puppy, choose a small harness with plenty of adjustment, but be aware that you will need to buy a larger harness as your dog grows.

Some harnesses have the additional feature of a seatbelt attachment, which is one option if you are traveling with your dog in the car. This is discussed in Chapter 10. You will need to decide on your preferred method of transporting your dog, but most people find a crate in the hatch to be the safest and most practical option. This can be your dog's indoor crate, but if the budget will stretch to it, a separate crate for the car will be more convenient in the long run.

When choosing your crate or crates, it goes without saying your dog will grow in size considerably if you are buying a puppy. However, a medium-sized crate is generally large enough for a Springer Spaniel. They do actually find comfort in a space that is not unnecessarily large, so you don't have to feel you need to buy the biggest crate in the store; you can leave these for the Mastiff owners. A metal crate is the best choice for a puppy as he is likely to chew a fabric crate.

Probably the most exciting bit of shopping for your new dog is choosing his bed, but if you are expecting a puppy, a plain plastic bed is the most sensible option. This is because your dog is highly likely to destroy his bed very quickly if it is made from stuffed textile material. You should wait until he is beyond the puppy stage before investing in the luxury option. A plastic bed will also contain any accidents while your dog is still learning to control his bladder. You can make it comfortable with old blankets or towels which can be easily washed. He will be perfectly happy with this. As with the crate, the bed does not need to be huge. Your puppy will feel comfort from being enclosed and will settle more readily.

You will need bowls for your dog's food and water, and these should ideally be made from heavy earthenware to prevent spilling or being pushed around the kitchen floor. There is a design of bowl available specifically for Spaniels with their long floppy ears, and this is narrower at the top than the bottom, the idea being that the ears remain outside the bowl and do not get covered in food or water. If you find you have a dog that bolts his food, you may also consider a greedy-feeder bowl, which has raised prongs molded into the base that the dog has to eat around, and this can slow down a greedy dog considerably, resulting in less air intake and consequent gas problems.

Your English Springer Spaniel is a long-haired breed. He also has an undercoat that is prone to shedding. He will require regular grooming, as discussed in Chapter 13. To start off with, you should purchase a double-sided metal comb with a handle and a brush with wire bristles. You may also wish to buy nail clippers and round-ended scissors. If you find later that he gets hot but you do not wish to clip him, a Furminator tool can thin the undercoat.

If you have carpets in your home, one of the best investments you can make is the purchase of a carpet shampooer. This will enable you to deal with the inevitable accidents your puppy will have calmly and without fuss. It will maintain the hygiene of your home, and ensure that no ammonia smell remains in the carpet that can encourage repeat soiling.

If you are concerned about the expense of all the things your new dog is likely to need, remember, your dog has no concept of what his new belongings have cost. There is no need to pay extra for designer items unless you particularly wish to. Your dog's accessories do not even have to be new, as long as any secondhand items have been thoroughly cleaned and disinfected. Your dog will quickly outgrow many of his first set of belongings, and will probably destroy the rest, so there will be considerably less tension between you if you have not spent a lot of money at the outset. When he is fully grown, his adult teeth have come in, and he is more sensible, then is the time to invest in better quality items that will have greater longevity and that your dog may appreciate.

Preparing for the arrival of a new dog is quite like preparing for the arrival of a baby! It is exciting, but when the time comes, there may be good times and bad times, and things you did not expect. As long as you have done some research, set your expectations at a realistic level, and are prepared for a bit of flexibility, then there is every reason that your new dog will instantly feel at home, and you will wonder if there was ever a time when he wasn't a part of the family.

Photo Courtesy of
Billy McKechnie

# CHAPTER 5
# How to Choose an English Springer Spaniel

Once you have decided the breed for you is an English Springer Spaniel, the first decisions may seem to be, male or female, liver and white or black and white? But although these are fundamental considerations, they are just a matter of preference, and neither gender nor color are a factor in what makes for a good dog, and the right fit for you. You may even completely change your mind on both counts when you connect with a particular dog.

So where should you look for your new dog? And once you have a breeder or shelter in your sights, what should you be looking for in the dog that is to share your life? This chapter will guide you through these decisions, to help you avoid the pitfalls, and be sure that the dog that comes home with you is the best fit for your future together.

# Purchasing or Rescuing?

*"Rescue dogs need homes as well, but patience is required because most of the circumstances were not of their (the dogs) doing. Most of these dogs need love, understanding training and socialization."*

**Dawn Horock**
*Daz-End English Springer Spaniels*

The English Springer Spaniel is a pedigree dog that comes with a fairly high price tag. If not, there will be a reason. The Springer Spaniel can be a complex breed, and sometimes puppies are chosen with no forethought, or the owner finds they cannot commit to the demands of the breed. These dogs that have been let down find themselves in rescue, many with issues that were not initially of their making. Or you may see a private advertisement for a dog needing a good home, and feel drawn to its plight. You may feel that when there are unwanted dogs in the world, the right thing to do is to consider rescue first. This is a noble intention, as long as you are prepared for potentially rehabilitating a damaged or untrained dog, or taking a dog with health issues. If you have the experience, and can fully commit to this responsibility and possibly extra financial cost over the dog's lifetime, then it can be very rewarding to adopt a dog from a rescue center.

It is important to note that rescue centers do not give their dogs away for free. There will always be an adoption fee of several hundred dollars. This is to cover some of the dog's expenses, but also to ensure that the dog is taken for the right reasons by an owner who is prepared to commit to it. Otherwise rescue dogs would be taken for profit or dog fighting. Rescue dogs are almost always neutered to prevent further breeding.

If you have not owned a Springer Spaniel before, and especially if you are a new dog owner, then there are good reasons why you might start out by buying a puppy from a breeder.

**FUN FACT**

English Springer Rescue America

English Springer Rescue America (ESRA) is a 501(c)(3) nonprofit organization that aims to provide foster homes and ultimately rehome English Springers who end up at animal shelters. ESRA was incorporated in August 1999 and operates nationwide. Visit www.springerrescue.org for more information.

*Photo Courtesy of Carol Farmer*

It is a misconception that by buying a puppy, you are starting with a blank canvas. Your canvas is not entirely blank; it has been primed by the genetics of the dog that you buy. This will be discussed later in this chapter. However, any adult dog is the product of both nature and nurture, and the nurture component is in your hands when you start with a puppy. The first few months after you bring your puppy home are vital in setting him up for adult life, so as long as you know what will be expected of you in these early months and are prepared to put in the work, there is the best possible chance of turning out an excellent dog while forging a close bond between you right from the get-go.

Sometimes Springer Spaniel puppies will turn up in rescue, if, for instance, a pregnant Springer has found her way into the shelter, or a litter of newly born pups has been dumped (which is rare with a valuable pedigree breed). This may seem an ideal compromise for those who really want to rescue but don't have enough experience for an adult dog with issues. However, these puppies will come from unknown bloodlines and unknown parentage. They may be crossbreeds, and they may carry genetic conditions that will only become apparent later in their lives, so this needs to be considered if you have the opportunity to rescue a puppy.

In buying a puppy from a breeder, you have the assurance of taking on a known quantity. You will know the bloodlines and temperaments of the parents, you will know they do not carry any genetic health conditions, the puppies will have been whelped and weaned with close attention to their health, and they will have had appropriate contact with their mother and littermates during their first weeks of life. Your puppy will come to you having had veterinary checks, vaccinations, worming, and certification, and if you wish to show your dog, you have the pedigree certificate that you will need in order to register your dog with the Kennel Club in your country.

There is no right or wrong decision whether to purchase or adopt; it depends entirely on the owner's preference, experience, intentions, and finance. Whichever route you choose, at the end of the day, a lucky dog will be starting or restarting his life in a loving home.

# The Differences Between Working and Show Lines

The most important consideration in selecting an English Springer Spaniel is the distinction between working lines and show-bred or "bench" lines. The gene pools between these lines have been almost entirely segregated since the mid-twentieth century, and as a result, the divergence has resulted in two quite different sets of dogs. This fact is often completely overlooked by the prospective owner, and is the most significant contributor to Springer Spaniels being given up to rescue centers when their new home does not work out.

It is especially sad for a Springer Spaniel to be given up by its owner, as this breed bonds particularly closely with its primary caregiver. So although English Springer Spaniels are adaptable and capable of transferring their affections, it is initially stressful for a dog of this breed to lose the person to whom they have become attached.

Although most breeders will take a dog back if things do not work out, these dogs will have missed out on the vital early weeks of training and socialization that are important to set them up for adult life. And as it will usually be the more intense working dogs that are returned, they will have missed the early higher-level training they would have received, so they are at a disadvantage and less attractive to huntsmen. It is important that these dogs should not be let down by ensuring they go to the most appropriate homes from the outset. Many responsible breeders of working lines will only let their puppies go to homes where they will be worked.

On the other hand, not every dog from working lines will turn out to have an aptitude in the field, and these more sensitive dogs may adapt well to life as domestic pets, as they will have had some early training and social-ization. So situations may arise when an adult (or adolescent) working-bred dog is sold by a breeder as a pet, but as a general rule, owners looking for a dog to share family life should look at show lines.

Show-bred Springer Spaniels are different from their working cousins in both looks and temperament. In appearance, they are larger in size, less wiry, with a longer coat, longer ears, and a squarer muzzle. So even without a pedigree certificate, for example when a dog turns up in rescue, it is usu-ally possible to identify whether a Springer Spaniel is from working or show stock. Of course there may be some crossover where unregulated breeding has taken place.

If you intend to hunt with your Springer Spaniel, then you will be look-ing at working lines and for a puppy to forge that close working relation-ship and high level of training required of a gundog. A dog from working lines will have more stamina, higher energy, and greater athleticism than his show-bred cousin. However, he is still a dog that craves human compan-ionship, and will love to live in his owner's home given the chance, rather than the traditional gundog kennel.

This distinction is stressed throughout this book simply for the fact that it is so often overlooked, or because prospective owners choose a dog from working lines because they live in country houses. The most critical thing in choosing any dog is committing to caring for it for its whole life, barring un-foreseen circumstances. So the right fit is imperative. For this reason, un-derstanding the distinction between working and show lines is so important for the welfare of the dog.

Photo Courtesy of
Charles Phillips

# Researching the Establishment

*"Research and speak with others who have dealt with the rescue or breeder. I am the founder of the National Rescue Program so I have seen hundreds of dogs consistently from the same breeders who mass produce puppies and are not honest about their dogs, health, and temperament. Many of these internet breeders do not stand behind or work with owners when issues arise."*

**Judy Ann Manley**
*Vistah Kennels*

If you have decided to buy a puppy from a breeder, a very good place to start is with the Kennel Club in your country. The Kennel Club website will have a searchable database of breeders offering dogs for sale in your area, and you will have the reassurance that the breeder is approved and inspected. This means that your puppy will have been bred from quality breeding stock, clear of genetic health conditions, and from parents with superb temperaments. It means that the health and welfare of the parents, especially the mother, has been a priority as well as that of the puppies.

By choosing an approved Kennel Club breeder, you will know that you are encouraging responsible breeding and not falling into the trap of inadvertently buying from a backyard breeder or puppy mill. These breeders are unregulated and the mothers are often started too young, bred from continually and into their senior years. This is a welfare issue and will also impact on the health of the puppies. They may be bred with no regard for genetic problems, and not receive basic health care, screening, worming, and vaccinations before being separated too early from the mother. If you see a litter of puppies advertised online, on a noticeboard, or in the newspaper, you may not make the association with a puppy mill, as the puppies are usually shown to prospective owners in a clean and tidy front room that is no indicator of the squalor around the back. You may even see the puppy with a female that is purported to be the mother, but may be a different dog. Apart from purchasing an unknown quantity in terms of bloodlines and future health conditions, you will not be able to show an unregistered dog in conformation classes if that is something you might like to do in the future. But being aware of puppy mills is a welfare issue above all else.

If you already know any English Springer Spaniels whose temperaments appeal to you, it is worth asking the owners about the bloodlines of their dog, and the breeder who produced the dog. Bloodlines are generally a reliable indicator of what to expect in an adult dog, and whereas all dogs have their own unique character, especially Springer Spaniels, broadly speaking you will have a better idea of what you are buying. You may of course have to wait for a litter to become available, but registering an interest with a breeder will mean you are notified when the time comes.

If you are purchasing a dog from working stock with the intention of participating in field trials, you will stand the best chance of competing at this level if you buy from a breeder with proven dogs. Likewise, if you wish to show your dog, you need to look for bloodlines that have done well in conformation classes.

# Inquiring about the Parents

If you are adopting an English Springer Spaniel from a rescue, you are not likely to have any information about the parents. This is due to the fact many dogs find themselves in rescue with no background information. But in the case of those that do come with pedigree papers, these are usually held back to protect the anonymity of the previous owner. Nevertheless, any genetic conditions known to the rescue will always be communicated to the adopter.

In all other cases, it is important to inquire about the parents of the puppy you are considering. This is because the dog will inherit elements of both parents in its temperament, conformation, field abilities, and overall health. If the breeder seems to be withholding any information when asked about the parents, it is time to walk away.

You should make certain that the mother of your puppy is over 20 months of age and has not produced a previous litter within the past 12 months. If you require Kennel Club registration for your dog, this will not be provided if the mother has already had 4 litters or is over the age of 8 years. She should also not have had more than two previous caesarian sections, and the puppies should not be the product of mating between father/daughter, mother/son, or brother/sister. Usually, the father will come from a different breeder, which keeps the gene pool clear of the problems caused by incestuous breeding.

You should always be able to see the mother of the puppies, who will be with the litter if they are not yet weaned. You may reasonably ask to make an appointment to see the father also if he is kept elsewhere. A copy of his pedigree certificate in any case should be available to view from the owner of the mother.

When you look at a litter of puppies, the only reliable indicator of what they will look like as adults is the appearance of the parents. If you cannot see the father in person, the breeder should be able to show you a photograph. Look for good proportions, especially if you intend to show your dog.

## Genetic testing

Both parents should have been screened and scored prior to mating to ensure they are not carriers of the inherited conditions that can affect English Springer Spaniels.

Kennel Club Assured Breeders are required to test for Acral Mutilation Syndrome (AMS), Fucosidosis (FUCO), Progressive Retinal Atrophy (PRA), Goniodysgenesis/Glaucoma (G), and Phosphofructokinase deficiency (PFK). The British Kennel Club lists dogs on their website that have tested clear or have carrier status.

Dogs that have tested clear have no copies of the mutant gene, and their offspring will be unaffected.

Dogs that have tested as carriers have one copy of the mutant gene, and one normal gene. The normal gene ensures that they do not suffer from the condition, but they have a 50% chance of passing on the mutant gene to each puppy.

Dogs that have two copies of the mutant gene are classed as affected. They will develop the disease and should never be bred from. Their offspring would either be affected or carriers, depending on the status of the other parent.

Carrier status dogs will appear to be unaffected, but if a backyard breeder produces a litter from two carrier parents, there is only a 25% chance any puppy will be clear. There is a 50% chance any puppy will be a carrier, and a 25% chance any puppy will be affected. Registered breeders may breed from one carrier parent as long as the other parent is clear. In this case, there is a 50% chance any puppy will be clear, and a 50% chance any puppy will be a carrier, but will not go on to develop the condition.

The scores in which most potential buyers are especially interested are those for hip and elbow dysplasia, which is discussed in Chapter 15. Springer Spaniels can be affected by this hereditary condition where the hip socket or elbow joint develops abnormally, making the joint unstable. This will lead to lameness as early as young adulthood and arthritis later on. It is heartbreaking to see an active dog like an English Springer Spaniel in pain, and corrective surgery is extremely expensive, so it stands to reason that owners are on their guard for this potential future problem.

*Photo Courtesy of
Tori Loudermilk*

Hip and elbow dysplasia tests are not DNA tests, but the scores are determined by X-ray after the age of one year. The X-rays are reviewed by a panel of official radiologists and orthopedic specialists and assessed by two scrutineers, for consistent application of the standard.

Hip dysplasia scores range from 0-106, which is an aggregate of the scores for both hips. The breed mean score for the English Springer Spaniel is 12.9, so the parents should both score lower than this.

Elbow dysplasia scores range from 0-3. Both elbows are graded, with the higher score being recorded. Breeding dogs should score 0.

# Looking at the Puppy

*"I have many people who only want a black/white pup or a liver/white pup. Color is irrelevant. I tell people it's like buying a new car. When you are shopping around color is a primary consideration, but after a few weeks you kind of forget about the color and what is under the hood becomes far more important. Like the old saying with horses goes, 'A good horse can't be a bad color'. Same goes for dogs."*

**Tim Whitney**
*ESS Breeder*

Going to look at a litter for the first time is very exciting. You may be expecting to form an instant bond with one of the littermates in particular, and know that he or she is destined to share your life. Or you may be worried about how to choose, and be uncertain what you should be looking for. Assuming you have done your homework and are going to see a litter of Kennel Club–registered English Springer Spaniels, you can be confident that any puppy you are offered has the best chance of a healthy life. Also, if you are looking for a pet you will be looking at dogs from show (bench) lines, and if you are looking to hunt with your dog, you will be choosing from a litter of working-line dogs. So you can be assured that although the puppies are a long way from revealing their adult personalities and potential, their bloodlines will predispose them to becoming the dog that is the best fit for you and your family.

A good time to visit the litter is when the pups are around six weeks old. By this time, it will be clear that the puppies are healthy and they will have begun to interact with each other and to be handled. Do check with the breeder if any of the puppies are already reserved. Often they will be wearing a colored collar, but with Springer Spaniels that have unique markings, this may serve sufficiently for identification. You don't want to set your heart on a puppy that turns out not to be available.

Your first impressions of the puppies' living environment is important. It should be clean and sufficiently spacious with clean water available, and the puppies themselves should be clean. Pay special attention to the back end for any signs of diarrhea. Are the puppies playing happily and confidently? Do they look well fed? They should have a healthy curiosity toward you.

Ask the breeder for permission to pick up each puppy in turn. They should be comfortable with being handled. If they are not, it may be an indication of a dominant puppy, or a more general sign that they have not been socialized. Check the puppy's eyes for discharge, and sniff their ears for infection. Have a look at the pup's mouth to check for healthy pink gums and a correct bite. The upper teeth should close over the lower teeth. Check the navel for an umbilical hernia, and the male pups for two descended testicles. If these are not apparent yet, they should have both dropped into the scrotum by eight weeks and by the time you collect your puppy.

By now, you will probably be feeling drawn to a particular puppy or at least to have narrowed your choice down. If you do not yet have a lot of Springer Spaniel experience, it is wise to choose neither the most active nor the quietest of the litter, but to aim for the middle ground. If you still can't choose, ask the breeder for advice. Their experience is ideal to draw upon in selecting the puppy most suited to your circumstances. In most cases, the breeder will want to be sure their puppy is going to a good home, so don't panic if you are asked questions yourself. After all, a caring breeder is just as invested in the puppy as you, his future owner.

When the puppy is 8-10 weeks old, you will be able to bring him home. And that is where the fun begins!

# Considerations of a Rescue Dog

*"If purchasing from a breeder, I recommend choosing one that has proven dogs. It is a poor choice to buy a dog with the intent of competing in field trials from someone whose dogs haven't proven their ability to compete at that level."*

**Greg Butler**
*Walnut Run Kennels*

It has already been mentioned that if you are adopting a dog from a rescue, in most cases you are taking on an unknown quantity in terms of genetics. However, if you are adopting an adult dog, his personality will have already developed. This can be useful, unless he has been emotionally damaged by past experiences. In these cases, you need to be a special person to help the dog rehabilitate. Many people find this challenge especially rewarding, if they have the compassion and resilience to handle it.

As your dog is unlikely to come with a pedigree certificate or any known parentage, it is wise to take out insurance for veterinary fees from day one. This will ensure that if the dog is going to develop genetic health conditions, such as hip or elbow dysplasia, you will be covered, as any condition for which the dog has been treated before cover was taken out will be excluded for life. These lifelong conditions can turn out to be extremely expensive, and if a dog does not have veterinary cover, most owners would not be able to afford thousands of dollars for an operation that could radically improve their dog's quality of life.

If you are adopting an elderly dog, some insurers will not issue policies for dogs over a certain age, usually eight years. However, others will accept dogs of any age, but the premiums will reflect the risk. Although the years ahead of you may be short, be prepared for heavy financial costs when taking on an elderly dog. Some rescue organizations will continue to fund or subsidize the veterinary costs of an older dog.

When you adopt from a rescue organization, any follow-up is usually on the part of the adopter letting the rescue know how well things are turning out, but the rescue takes on a lifetime commitment to the dog known as rescue backup (RBU). This means a reputable rescue will take the dog back if things do not work out, and the adopter cannot sell the dog or pass it on without permission from the rescue. This is to ensure no rescue dog ever falls into the wrong hands again in its lifetime.

Choosing your English Springer Spaniel is very exciting, but also something that should not be rushed into without considering the points raised in this chapter. But with a little background research under your belt, you will have the best chance of finding a canine partner that will slot right into your life and share many happy years ahead.

# CHAPTER 6
# **Behavioral Training**

The English Springer Spaniel is a highly intelligent breed, and one that really wants to please. These two breed traits automatically set you up for success when training a Springer Spaniel. However, they are also a very sensitive breed, often to the point of neuroticism. So, if you are adopting an older dog that has suffered some negative life experiences or has never been properly trained to live in a home, you may have ingrained behavioral issues to address. And if you are bringing home a puppy, the early months are vitally important to establish all the desired behaviors that will help him fit into family life. This chapter will deal with the three issues most owners are likely to experience: housebreaking, destructive behavior, and separation anxiety.

# Housebreaking

*"If the puppy has an accident, don't get upset or mean to the puppy. You have to be consistent with taking the puppy outside. It's not always fun for us, as owners to go outside when it's raining or really cold. As a puppy we have to be patient and set them up to win by providing adequate time for them to do their business."*

**Dawn Horock**
*Daz-End English Springer Spaniels*

If you have just brought home an English Springer Spaniel puppy, chances are that before you have even gotten through the door, he has already had an accident in the car (hopefully you have taken plenty of towels)! An 8-10 week old puppy does not yet have full bladder or bowel control, but he does already have some early concept of appropriate toileting learned from his mother, and an instinct not to soil his eating and sleeping area. This is something you will build upon in housebreaking your new puppy so that as he develops physical control, he also learns the acceptable place to potty.

Because your new puppy will inevitably have accidents in the home, however diligent you are in his training, it is important never to punish him. This is because Springer Spaniels are a sensitive breed and by causing him anxiety, it will make the situation worse. If you have hard floors, this is an advantage as the mess can be quickly and thoroughly cleaned up. If you have carpets, and have taken the advice given in Chapter 4 and invested in a carpet shampooer, this gadget may become your second-best friend in the months to come, as prompt and thorough cleaning of soiled areas is important. This is because any residual odor sends a message to the dog that this is an approved toileting spot. You should also be sure to use a pet-specific ammonia-neutralizing cleaning product, as many general household cleaners contain ammonia and encourage toileting in the cleaned area as they smell like urine to the dog.

**FUN FACT**

**English Springer Spaniel Field Trial Association (ESSFTA)**

The ESSFTA is recognized by the AKC as the "parent club" for the English Springer Spaniel breed. This means that the ESSFTA maintains the breed standard as well as sets the rules for English Springer Spaniel breed-specific performance events in America.

Photo Courtesy of
Carol Farmer

So, in having your cleaning strategies in place, you will be feeling calm and patient about housebreaking your puppy. This is important, as the positive reinforcement approach works best with most dogs, and in particular with English Springer Spaniels.

If you have adopted an adult dog that appears not to be housebroken, the same methods can be used as if you were training a puppy. But in most cases, your adult dog does have bladder and bowel control. So, you may be working harder on correcting ingrained negative behavior, but you do not have the issue of physical control to deal with.

Most trainers advocate the use of a crate when housebreaking a puppy. In introducing your dog to a crate that is his safe space, and the place where he sleeps at night and rests during the day, he instinctively does not wish to soil it. Therefore, he will exercise what physical control he has in refraining from toileting in his crate. Obviously with a puppy, this is physically quite challenging, so the owner should take the dog outside very frequently to do his business. You may find that your dog favors a particular area to relieve himself in the yard, and his scent will draw him back to this area repeatedly. You can use this observation to your advantage by taking him to his favored spot in the reliable expectation that he will relieve himself there promptly. When your dog is actually in the act of squatting or raising his hind leg, then is the time to use your chosen command word. This may be "busy," "potty," or any word of your choosing. Your dog will make the association between the word and the act, and in time, as the word becomes ingrained in his consciousness, and when he develops physical control, you can use the word to command the act.

You should not use your chosen command word in the early stage of housebreaking at any point, apart from when the dog is actually relieving himself, so that the word is associated with the act of toileting, and not with running around the yard doing his own thing!

As your puppy's physical control develops, you will notice there are certain times when he needs to relieve himself, and you can use these times to reinforce his housebreaking training. These are on first waking up in the morning, around 5 to 30 minutes after eating, and after playing. The more times you can take your dog outside to toilet and achieve a correct behavior, the more the behavior becomes learned and ingrained. Conversely, if you do not give your dog adequate opportunity to go outside, and he has repeated accidents in the house, it will set back your training. It is not fair for a young puppy to be left in his crate or in the house for many hours while the owner is out at work, as he will have toileting accidents and feel stressed by them.

Remember to make lots of fuss over your dog for doing the right thing once he has completed toileting outside. Don't distract him in the act, but once he has finished, make sure he knows how good he is. You can also give him a small treat. Your Springer Spaniel is so keen to please you, he will love the attention and learn very quickly that appropriate toileting is what is required of him.

Some owners like to use clicker training with their dogs. With this method, at the specific point of a correct behavior (in this case, completing the toileting act outside), the owner clicks the clicker, then rewards the dog with a treat or fuss. If you are retraining an adult dog, clicker training can help with focusing the dog's attentions, as the click is very positive and consistent.

Housebreaking an English Springer Spaniel is not usually difficult; however, you may sometimes encounter problems even after the dog seems to have gotten it.

Some puppies may continue to suffer urinary incontinence when they are excited, especially when you greet them when returning home. This is usually a phase they will grow out of by the time they are a year old. In the meantime, you should anticipate the act by taking your puppy outside into a safe area as soon as you open the door, so that any involuntary urination does not soil your home. It is not your puppy's fault and will not impact on their housebreaking understanding.

Another form of involuntary urination is submissive urination, which is accompanied by a submissive posture such as tail tucking, crouching or rolling onto their back. Most puppies will outgrow this behavior as their confidence develops, so they should never be scolded, as this will set them back. You will need to be very sensitive to your dog if he is especially insecure, training him gently and positively and establishing a routine. Dominance training, where the owner assumes a pack-leader position, will be counterproductive with a very submissive dog.

Some dogs may urinate inside the home deliberately as an act of marking. This is often in response to another animal in the house or within sight of a window. Or the dog might be reacting to the presence of a child in the house, or even an adult houseguest that the dog perceives as a challenge. Marking behavior can quickly become an established pattern. If your dog is old enough, neutering usually reduces the behavior. If it persists, you will need to look at other ways to address the problem. For example, always cleaning the marked areas promptly with an ammonia-neutralizing product, as mentioned previously, and addressing conflict with other household pets or children. You may also consider restricting the dog's access to the areas he marks, or making the marked areas unattractive to soiling by feeding the dog in that spot or placing his bed there.

If your dog is still soiling indoors, he or she may have a physical problem, so you should take your dog to your veterinarian for a checkup. If your dog is an older female, especially if she has been spayed, she may develop urinary incontinence in her senior years, but the good news is that this is treatable with medication. In other cases, anti-anxiety medication may help stress-incontinence and marking behaviors.

# Chewing and Destructive Behavior

*"Like all new puppies, English Springer Spaniel's do go through the teething stage. They like to chew on things. For the first couple months I would recommend picking up anything you do not want to get chewed on."*

**Ahavah Tindell**
*Aquilla Creek Farms*

Puppies love to chew, and in fact it is a natural and necessary behavior. During your dog's first year, he will go through two developmental stages in his chewing. Puppy teething takes place between three and seven months of age, during which the dog has an uncontrollable urge to chew. This relieves discomfort and helps the shedding of their puppy teeth. Chewing also assists the eruption of the adult teeth from seven months onward, after which your dog may go through a period of adolescent chewing as the adult teeth set into the jawbone. The whole first year of a puppy's life can be very uncomfortable due to the teething process, and chewing gives him some relief. It also satisfies his natural curiosity by allowing him to explore new textures as his world unfolds.

The key to successfully managing your puppy's urge to chew is to redirect his behavior toward acceptable and safe items, and away from the things in your house that you do not wish to see destroyed. There should be a distinction between toys and chews. Toys, even those designed for dogs, are not indestructible and are not designed for intentional chewing, so they should always be put away after use while your dog is a puppy for his own safety. Chews are safe for gnawing and will not fall apart or splinter. Your dog will enjoy a natural chew, such as a deer's antler, pig's ear, or pizzle, or a manufactured chew toy such as a Nylabone® or a rubber Kong®. This has a cavity inside that can be packed with cream cheese, pate, dog food, or peanut butter (check the label that the peanut butter does not contain xylitol). Be aware that not all chew products marketed at dogs are necessarily safe. Cooked bones should never be given as they may splinter, and rawhide can be swallowed and cause a blockage. It is often also heavily chemically treated. It is recommended that your dog should be supervised when given a consumable chew to gnaw on, although non-consumable chews such as Nylabones® or Kongs® can be useful to leave with your dog when you go out.

*Photo Courtesy of Rebecca Panayi*

Your dog likes variety and may become bored with the same chew, so it's a good idea to have a selection of chews, and to rotate them to maintain your dog's interest.

Appropriate chewing should always be rewarded with praise. Your dog should not be scolded for inappropriate chewing, but a firm "No" along with removal of the item should soon establish a connection in your Springer Spaniel's intelligent mind, as to which items he is and is not allowed to chew.

Some dogs may be discouraged from inappropriate chewing by means of a product called "Bitter Apple." This is a spray that can be applied to items your dog may have taken a liking to, such as chair legs, and the unpleasant taste will deter him.

Chews are not just for puppies. Even when your dog is an adult and no longer feels discomfort from teething, chewing is still a natural behavior and keeps his teeth clean. Thus, he should have access to appropriate chews throughout his life.

If your dog is destructive in the house, pulling the stuffing out of your sofa or destroying your slippers for example, this behavior may be a part of his chewing instinct as he explores the world, but it may also be because he is bored. Providing appropriate chews will help on both counts, but leaving a puppy uncrated while you go out is allowing him unrestricted opportunity to explore and destroy anything left within his reach. His anxiety may also add to his destructive behavior, as will be discussed in the next section. This is one reason why crate-training your puppy from the outset is a good idea. He is more likely to settle and be less anxious in his safe place, and not have access to household items. Therefore, there is less risk of spiraling inappropriate behavior. The more control you have over your puppy's early training, the more effective it will be.

# Separation Anxiety

Separation anxiety can be a real issue for English Springer Spaniels. They are a sensitive breed prone to anxiety, and they form a very close bond with their owner. Working Springers are often fortunate enough to go everywhere with their owner, and the constant exercise also helps to exhaust them physically so that they can settle on their own. Domestic Springers, however, often need to be left while their owner goes to work or to the shops. Springer Spaniels from working lines are more intense and energetic than their show-bred cousins, and in previous chapters there was an emphasis on selecting from the more placid show lines for a domestic pet. Any Springer, though, may suffer from separation anxiety, as companionship is in their nature. Preempting the problem by early conditioning is essential.

Separation anxiety may manifest itself by howling or barking in your absence, and often by destructive behavior. The dog may pace, pant, drool, whine, and remain unsettled for the whole time you are gone, and on your return may cry pitifully. To him, you have just returned from the dead. You knew you were coming back. He did not. You need to build his trust by gradually increasing the time you are gone, so he knows that your absence is not the end of his world.

To your dog, being separated is a big deal. You need him to know that it is not. He will read and interpret your body language, so when you leave your dog, do it without fanfare. When you return, try to ignore his crying and exuberant attentions. Ignore him completely for a few minutes until he has calmed down, and then give him some gentle fuss. When you first start conditioning your dog to being left alone, you should not even leave the house. Just shut the door on him for a few minutes, and then return. Try not to return while he is howling, but pick a moment when he is quiet, to convey the right message. This way he is rewarded for the desired behavior. As you build up the time you leave him, you can adopt a mock routine, maybe putting on your coat and picking up your bag. But keep both the exit and the return low key so he knows it is nothing to get worked up about.

Once you are actually leaving the house, you will not know if your dog is howling. You may wish to install a Wi-Fi camera to monitor your dog's behavior in your absence. You may even find it reassuring to know that your dog has actually settled down, and is not shredding the carpet.

Puppies that have been crate-trained are likely to feel less anxious by confinement rather than the opposite, as they have their safe space, and have no expectations placed upon them such as guarding the house, so this can have a calming effect on their mind.

Photo Courtesy of Sandy Caughron

If you have adopted a Springer Spaniel that suffers from separation anxiety, you may have a bigger task on your hands in retraining his behavior than in conditioning a puppy. Rescue dogs often have suffered traumatic experiences in their past, and in finding you, they never want to let you out of their sight and be abandoned again. Rescue organizations are usually aware of dogs that suffer from separation anxiety and will not place them with an owner who is going to be out of the house for any length of time. Sometimes a damaged dog cannot be left at all. In these cases, patient and sympathetic rehabilitation is the only approach, and success is not guaranteed. The methods described for leaving a puppy can be tried, but if the dog is severely stressed, it may be necessary to adapt household patterns or employ a dogsitter so the dog is never or rarely alone. Some dogs may respond well to another canine companion of a placid nature.

It is always worth ensuring that your dog has had sufficient physical exercise before leaving him, has emptied his bladder, and that a radio or the television is left on to distract from any noises outside the home that may make him feel stressed. Some owners of anxious dogs find pheromone products useful. DAP, or Dog Appeasing Pheromone, mimics the calming scent of the dog's mother, and is available as a plug-in, spray, or infused collar. In more severe cases, the vet can prescribe calming medication.

Four hours is the maximum time a dog should be left alone even if he is well adjusted and does not suffer separation anxiety. At this point he needs a comfort break. Owners that work longer hours should make arrangements for their dog to be let out during this time, but Springer Spaniels generally need human company, and do not do well being left for long periods. This consideration should be kept in mind when deciding on a Springer Spaniel for a pet, as no breed will love you and want to be with you more.

If this is your first dog, it may seem daunting to have responsibility for your dog's behavioral development and emotional welfare. But you should never feel you have to do this alone. In fact, both you and your dog can benefit from puppy classes if they are available in your area. Having guidance and support from an experienced trainer will encourage and direct you as an owner, and your dog will gain a lot from socializing with other dogs. Also, if you are adopting an older dog, or continue to experience problems as your puppy develops, you should never be afraid to seek the advice of a professional behaviorist who can assess your individual dog, rather than relying on generic solutions on the internet. Some rescue organizations have their own behaviorists to provide ongoing support. English Springer Spaniels each have their own unique characters. Most will learn quickly and settle into their new lives, others may struggle. Those that do not adapt as readily may be experiencing a wide variety of issues, and a behaviorist who really understands the breed will be in the best position to identify these and suggest strategies to help your dog.

For most English Springer Spaniels, behavioral issues are just a phase of puppyhood, that can be worked through with a bit of patience and understanding. Whether you are conditioning a puppy or retraining an adult dog, working toward desirable behavior will strengthen your bond, create a happier dog, and give the greatest sense of satisfaction when you begin to see the fruits of your endeavors.

# CHAPTER 7
# Recall

One of the things that appeals most about owning an English Springer Spaniel is the prospect of long walks in the countryside, taking in the fresh air and scenery, while your dog enjoys the scents he finds in the bushes and the opportunity to stretch his legs—always staying close by while you get some valuable exercise together.

This is the expectation, but the reality may be completely different!

This chapter will outline why recall is so important for the English Springer Spaniel, and give you some tips on how to achieve it.

# The Importance of Recall for the English Springer Spaniel

In Chapter 2 of this book, it was explained that the English Springer Spaniel has a long heritage as a hunting dog, and for nearly two thousand years the breed changed relatively little. It is only in the last century that the bloodlines of the Springer Spaniel have diverged into working and show lines, but even the show-bred dogs have hunting in their blood. Therefore, any English Springer Spaniel has a set of instincts that are part of his DNA, and top of the list is his hunting drive.

Whether you actually wish to hunt with your dog, or simply enjoy off-leash walks in open countryside, the most important thing is that you can call your dog back. This should be easy, right? After all, the English Springer Spaniel is intelligent, and he loves to be with his owner. Why would he even think about running off? The thing to recognize with an English Springer Spaniel is that his hunting instinct is so strong, it is not controlled by his rational brain that loves you and knows you fill his food bowl. If he catches sight of a rabbit or pheasant, he simply cannot help himself, it has to be chased. This may be for a half mile, or through dense woodland, well out of your sight. If he loses one prey animal, he may lock onto another. He has no thought for returning to you as all his enjoyment synapses are firing relentlessly in his brain, blocking any other consideration. When eventually the game is over, he may be miles away. Chances are, his sense of direction is sufficient to locate you again, but in his own time, by which you may be frantic and have visions of your dog disappearing over the edge of a precipice or under the wheels of a vehicle, or shot by a protective farmer, any of which are possible.

This is not an enjoyable way to walk your dog, and definitely not what you signed up for when you brought home a Springer Spaniel. The good news is, if you have started with a puppy, recall can be taught, and those long relaxing walks can be achieved. The key to preventing bad habits, such as unbridled feral instincts, from taking hold is to stop them before they start. In the early weeks your puppy will

## STORY
### Go Fetch

A rescued English Springer Spaniel named Sam works at Otis Hardware in Spokane, Washington. His job is to carry small items to the cashier for customers. After years of training, Sam learned that he would earn a treat every time he brought an item from a customer to the front counter. He is now an eager and beloved fixture at the store.

Photo Courtesy of Rebecca Panayi

be happy to trot along happily beside you, his protector. It is only some-where between three and six months that his hunting drive kicks in, and this is where you need a hard focus on recall training with a Springer Span-iel, whether working or show-bred.

It may seem a bit harsh and unkind to curb your Springer Spaniel's natu-ral instincts. In fact, if you intend to hunt with your dog, you may even argue that you want to encourage his prey drive. This is not the case. The most important factor in hunting is control, and your dog has sufficient natural in-stinct to hunt without it being encouraged as a puppy. Experienced hunters will advocate keeping working-bred puppies away from wildlife during their first year, as the first accidental flush will fry their brain. The same advice is recommended for owners of show-bred pets, even though their prey-drive is not quite as intense as that of their working cousins.

So, whereas recall is important for any dog, for the English Springer Spaniel it is vital. Failure to achieve it during your dog's first year is setting him up to become a problem dog. A dog with no reliable recall cannot be walked off-leash for his own safety, which is severely restrictive and affects the amount of exercise your dog will get, as well as his natural enjoyment in his surroundings. It affects his interactions with other dogs, as a leash pre-vents free movement and can encourage aggression. It also makes it diffi-cult to leave your dog with a pet sitter or dog walker. And a dog walked off-leash with no recall may stray and fall into the wrong hands, or meet with an accident. All of these reasons and more make recall training the highest priority for English Springer Spaniel owners.

# How to Teach Recall

Teaching recall is not simply a matter of going for a walk and calling your dog back periodically for a biscuit. This is recall reinforcement, and very valuable, but it is secondary to actual recall training, which is a struc-tured and purposeful activity.

In fact, some trainers say that you should give up the idea of walking your dog as a puppy, and that every outing should be focused on training. There is much to be said for this idea, as young puppies should not be phys-ically overworked due to their growing bones and joints. And their concen-tration span is short, so keeping training sessions short but frequent will keep a puppy focused. This way the lesson sinks in, and he feels sufficiently mentally exhausted to settle down in the interim periods.

To your puppy, you need to be the center of his world. Springer Span-iels usually bond closely with their primary caretaker, so you are off to a good start. But you need to make time for him, interacting with, encour-aging, and playing with him as well as meeting his basic care needs. In this way, teaching recall has already begun, because your puppy will always be looking to you for his cues, and his attention will be on you when he is off-leash. This being said, as soon as you get into a more stimulating area than your own back yard, you will have to work harder at maintaining your dog's attention, as you are competing with his natural curiosity and the sights and scents of the countryside or park.

Your puppy should soon recognize his name, and this will help to get his attention, along with the command "Come," to bring him back to you. Reward his correct behavior with a small treat such as a biscuit, training treat, or dried liver chip. Give him some fuss, and then send him away again. This is like a game to your playful puppy, and he will love to gain your approval, not to mention the treat! You should start at this basic level in your own back yard or an enclosed space before venturing elsewhere, and never near a road in the early stages.

Some owners, especially those who intend to hunt, like to train their dog to the whistle. This has the advantage of carrying a long way if your dog is far from you. If you regularly walk your dog in popular dog-walking areas, however, multiple owners using whistles may confuse him. In this case, teaching a particular whistle pattern is a good idea.

The most effective way to keep your dog's attention on you when faced with multiple distractions is to keep changing direction. Don't allow your dog to predict where you are both going, or he will run on ahead. A zigzag path will keep him focused. This also mirrors the quartering pattern your dog will adopt if he is to hunt later on. Even if hunting is your ambition, and you have an end goal of sending your dog out quite long distances, teaching heel work at this stage sets the foundation, and tells your dog that the place to be is by your side, unless he has been given permission to go further away from you.

If all this training doesn't seem to you like it is fun for your dog, be reassured that he is actually loving having your complete attention, and by restricting his freedom now, you are permitting him greater freedom in adult life as a well-trained dog. But you should still allow your dog to enjoy using his nose and exploring his surroundings. And your Springer Spaniel has a natural talent for retrieving, so playing fetch also reinforces recall training. This is because he is focused on the ball or toy so he is not running off, and he is bringing it back to you. You should not overexert a puppy, but ending the session with a game serves the dual purpose of a lesson and a reward. It also increases the growing bond between you and your dog.

Photo Courtesy of
Nicola Lancaster

# Recall Problems and How to Solve Them

The advice given previously concerns training a puppy; however, the same techniques apply if you have taken on an adult dog with poor recall. You should always try the positive reinforcement approach first with a Springer Spaniel, as their natural inclination is to please you. However, an adult dog has ingrained behaviors that can be more challenging to retrain, so you should keep your off-leash sessions to a safe enclosed area while he is learning recall.

Whereas most Springer Spaniels form very strong attachments to their owner and indeed to any human, occasionally you may get a dog that has no social drive. In these cases, the dog feels no need for human company, and certainly nothing to draw him back from the thrill of his hunting drive. If your dog turns out to be psychologically wired in this way, or if you find you have taken on an adult dog with an established chase drive, you may find that the soft approach is getting you nowhere, and you may have to resort to more forceful training. This approach was used traditionally with working dogs, and although it has fallen out of favor in modern times, it still has its place where positive reinforcement has failed. In this case it is worth getting some professional help, at least to start you off.

Photo Courtesy of
Belinda Jayne Macleod

One more forceful training method is the use of an e-collar, favored by huntsmen. This is not an electric shock collar, as it does not zap the dog in a painful way, but it does emit a light stimulus via remote control to divert the dog's attention from the hunt and signal the need to return. The e-collar should only be used with a full understanding of how to operate it humanely.

If you have a Springer Spaniel with a high prey drive, it is a mistake to leave him outside unsupervised. He is highly likely to abscond, especially if he is kept with another dog, as there is nothing a highly driven dog likes to do more than hunt with a buddy. Any farmer is within his right to shoot a dog worrying his livestock. So, where recall cannot be achieved, the dog needs to be kept indoors, and always supervised outdoors.

If your puppy previously had an excellent recall and suddenly becomes defiant at around the age of nine months and challenges the boundaries by running off and doing his own thing, do not panic; this unfortunately is adolescence. However, for a while, you will have to take a step backward, and reinforce all the old recall training that seemed to be established. You may even have to walk your dog on a leash for a few months while he goes through this phase. This is for his safety, but also so that he does not get away with negative behavior which may consequently become ingrained. You may also consider the use of a training leash. These are very long lines that allow your dog to run, and for you to reestablish calling him back, without the danger of him going out of range. You should always attach a training leash onto a harness and not a collar, so that your dog does not run to the end of the line and get a sharp jolt to the neck. Your end of the line does not even need to be held, but it may be caught if necessary, to bring the dog back.

Another fun way to reinforce your bond and focus your dog is Canine Agility. Although this is not direct recall training, it does teach your dog to look to you for his cues the whole time, which will improve his recall out on his walks. Agility cannot be started while your dog is very young, as impact activities may damage his growth plates, but the potentially challenging adolescent stage at around nine months is also the point where he is physically able to start Agility. Having a fun job to do may see him through this period, and you will both emerge fit and focused! Agility and Flyball are discussed in Chapter 9.

Recall training is the most valuable, life-enhancing, and potentially life-saving lesson you can teach your Springer Spaniel, and it may all fall into place very easily, or it may present an ongoing challenge. Whatever your experience, you should never be afraid of taking a step backwards and returning to basics. You should have realistic expectations about walking your dog in his first year, with an emphasis on training rather than leisure. And if you feel you are getting nowhere, seek the help of a professional behaviorist. A bit of advice in the early stages is a worthwhile investment for the future, and those pleasurable walks in the countryside that you envisaged at the outset.

*Photo Courtesy of
Billy McKechnie*

# CHAPTER 8
# Socialization

One of the most endearing qualities possessed by the English Springer Spaniel is their love for humans, and the strong bond they form with their owner. By nature, they are friendly dogs with adults, children, other dogs, and, if correctly introduced, other family pets. However, the early months are very important in teaching social skills to your new puppy, as he learns how to fit into family life. This chapter will help you get on the right track from the start, so that your dog's affable, loving character develops just as expected of an English Springer Spaniel.

# Importance of Socialization

Some Springer Spaniel owners refer to the breed as "Velcro® dogs." That is to say, they will remain stuck to your side wherever you go! So you would be entitled to assume that socialization will be no problem at all for your English Springer Spaniel. Indeed, from his own point of view, he may well love everything and everybody. But his natural exuberance may make him less welcome in certain situations, and he needs to learn a few rules in

**FUN FACT**
**First Dogs**

Several English Springer Spaniels have called the White House their home over the years. George H.W. Bush, the 41st president of the United States, owned an English Springer Spaniel named Millie during his time in office. During his first term, the 43rd president, George W. Bush, owned one of Millie's puppies, Spot Fletcher.

order to fit into his new social circle. Failure to socialize a Springer Spaniel puppy correctly could lead to him frightening the children, chasing the cat, jumping up at your houseguests, or even more dangerous situations like provoking aggression in other dogs. You may even end up with a dog that has a mistrust of humans. This is not typical of a Springer Spaniel, so when it occurs, it indicates a bad experience in early life. These dogs often end up in shelters, where they need careful rehabilitation.

This chapter deals mostly with socializing a puppy, but if you have adopted a rescue dog, the socialization procedure is much the same. It may go more quickly if your dog already has social skills in place, or it may take considerably longer if you have to rehabilitate a dog with socialization and trust issues. In fact, the rescue center will have assessed your dog already, and if he has these issues he should not have been placed in a home with children, other dogs, or cats, unless the adopter is extremely experienced. An adult dog may have ingrained behavior that could endanger a child or another pet, so in these cases, damaged dogs are best rehabilitated away from the things to which they are reactive.

The good news is, if you are starting with a puppy, the good nature characteristic of the English Springer Spaniel should mean socialization is never too challenging.

# When to Socialize Your New Dog

*"It is critical to give your new pup as much interaction as possible with new people, places, and other animals between 8 and 16 weeks of age."*

**Greg Butler**
*Walnut Run Kennels*

Your English Springer Spaniel has already started socialization classes before you even picked him up, and his instructor was his mom. Puppies learn a lot from their mother in the early weeks, as well as from interacting with their litter mates. Their mom will nurture them and correct them, and they will learn behavior patterns such as keeping their sleeping area clean. As they grow, they will also learn how to play with their siblings. When you take your puppy home, you take mom's role as their instructor, plus, all of a sudden, your puppy has no playmates. So continuity is critical in the socialization process, and the period from 8 to 16 weeks will set your dog on a path for life.

As with other behavioral training, adolescence at around nine months can be a time when your dog starts to challenge the boundaries. You should keep up the socialization training throughout the first year by giving your dog plenty of monitored interaction with other adults, children, and pets, but be ready to take a sterner line during adolescence if you do find your dog starting to behave out of character. It is only a phase. Most Springer Spaniels will sail through life befriending anybody and anything that comes their way, and their desire to please you will mean your consistent guidance is all that is needed to help them understand the rules.

# Introducing Your New English Springer Spaniel to Other Dogs

*"Set them up for success. Not every other dog is friendly. Keep them either with the same size animal, or one that is tested to be good with puppies. Puppies are annoying and they have sharp teeth. They will get corrections from adult dogs. So don't expect the older dog to think the new puppy is as cute as you do."*

**Janet Warner**
*Majic Kennels*

Your new English Springer Spaniel has come from a situation of close contact with his litter mates, and if he has parted from his mother, this will only have been recently. So he is already very comfortable in the company of other dogs. However, now he has to learn how to interact with dogs that he does not know—older dogs, dogs of a different breed, and dogs that have a different temperament from those he has experienced up to now.

If you already have a dog, you may be bringing your new puppy home in the full expectation that your resident dog will relish having a new play-mate! This may not be love at first sight. There are two issues at stake here. Your resident dog has his own territory and his own humans, and he may be reticent to share them with the upstart interloper. Plus, if he is an older dog, he is likely to find a puppy very exhausting and very disrespectful of his personal space. Managing these two concerns sensitively is paramount in getting your resident dog to accept the puppy.

If you have more than one resident dog, you will have another dimension to the dynamic, as the hierarchy will have to be reestablished over the coming months. However, both dogs already understand about sharing their humans and rubbing along with another dog in the house.

You may already have an idea how introducing your new dog is likely to go if you have had friends' dogs in your house. You will know how accepting your resident dogs are of canine visitors. Your resident dogs do not know from the outset that the new puppy is here to stay, so initial introductions may go no differently from canine house guests. There may be confrontations, however, in the early stages if the newcomer invades your resident dogs' space; for example, while they are eating or sleeping. Puppies are new to this, so it is your job to supervise at all times to start off with. But a rebuke from your resident dog toward the puppy is all part of the learning process, much as he received from his mom, and the owner shouldn't be alarmed at confrontation as long as they are aware of the warning signs of genuine aggression. These are snarling, rigidity, and drawing back the gums. This is when your puppy needs to be removed from the situation for his safety.

Crate training your puppy is a good idea, to give him a safe space, and the resident dog or dogs time out away from the attentions of a non-stop exuberant puppy.

When you first bring home your puppy or your adult rescue dog, you should take your resident dog outside the home and only bring him back in after the new dog is already in the house. Allow the new dog's initial excitement to subside first. For the resident dog to go into the house and find the new dog already settled in place is less threatening than bringing the newcomer through the front door with all the fanfare this involves. It is a good idea for further introductions to take place in the yard where your resident dog will be less territorial, and both dogs are not confined to a small space.

The other aspect of socializing your new dog with other dogs involves dogs that belong to other people. It is very important for your new dog to widen his social circle as soon as he has completed his first vaccinations. You should ask your vet if they hold puppy classes at the practice. If not, they will be able to recommend one in the area. This is an ideal opportunity for you to introduce your puppy to other puppies at a similar stage in their development. It is a much safer way to socialize a puppy than in a public space with unknown adult dogs. Your puppy needs positive experiences in his early months or he may grow up with fear issues. You may get to know other puppy owners with whom you could meet socially outside of classes for puppy play dates. You will also have access to an experienced trainer who will give you support and advice during these vital first months.

Puppy classes often lead directly into obedience training classes, and it can be fun to continue your dog's training with the same set of dogs and owners.

While your dog is still a puppy, you should limit his interaction with older dogs, but introduce these experiences as he matures and starts to learn the rules. Set him up for success, and not failure, by ensuring his well-meaning attentions are always welcome, and never get him into trouble.

Dogs should greet each other by sniffing each end and wagging their tails. Be prepared to lead your puppy swiftly away from any initial contact with another dog if that dog should freeze for more than three seconds, as this may signal an impending attack.

Photo Courtesy of
Charles Phillips

If you have adopted a fearful dog you will need to take socialization very carefully to ensure all his interactions with other dogs are positive ones. Dog parks are not recommended for fearful dogs, as you can never be sure you will not encounter an aggressive dog to set your dog back. Walking a dog on the leash can also lead to an aggressive encounter as the on-leash dog or dogs feel anxious at being unable to get away. But on the other hand, a fearful dog, even if he has good recall, may bolt when off-leash. So you should keep your socialization opportunities to play dates with dogs that you know to be placid, in a private space, or away from crowded areas. This way, your fearful dog should eventually learn to trust other dogs, or at least, to have a few good friends.

# Introducing Your New English Springer Spaniel to Children

When you first select your puppy, it is an enormous advantage if the breeder has children of their own, and the litter has been raised in the home rather than a kennel. Kennel-raised dogs are also more likely to be from working lines, which are not recommended for families with young children, as they are more intense, exuberant, and outdoor-orientated. You should look for a puppy from show lines, and ideally raised in a family home.

As already noted, if you are adopting a rescue dog, the rescue organization will have already assessed the dog, usually in a foster home, to be certain that he is comfortable around children. Rescue organizations cannot risk sending an unassessed dog into a family home in case of an attack. Although English Springer Spaniels are not aggressive by nature, rescue dogs may be damaged by previous bad experiences, so they need to be rehomed responsibly. If you have adopted a dog that has been passed as safe with children, you are already well on your way. But you should still socialize your new dog carefully with your children, to ensure a happy relationship.

In the weeks leading up to collection of your new puppy or rescue dog, you should take your children to meet plenty of friendly, easygoing dogs belonging to friends and family, especially if you know any child-friendly English Springer Spaniels. Children can be quite wary of dogs as they seem much bigger to the child, who is looking into a mouth of sharp teeth at their eye-level. You should help your child to understand how to pet a dog and treat it with respect. Show your child how to stroke the dog gently on the back of its neck, and never to startle the dog with sudden movements. If your child is old enough, you can explain about body language, and how a dog is submitting to you if he rolls onto his back so you can stroke his tummy. But if he draws back his gums, he is saying he has had enough and it's time to leave him alone.

Once your dog is home, make sure that your child continues to respect his personal space, never petting him when he is eating or sleeping. And definitely never riding him like a pony! Older children should be brought on board with helping to look after the dog, giving him his meals and accompanying you on his walks. This helps the dog to know that the child is above him in the hierarchy. Problems can occur when the dog seeks to challenge the hierarchy for second place above the child. For this reason, if you have children, it is a bad idea to let the dog sleep on the adults' bed or even in their bedroom, as it tells the dog he is more important than the child, and the adults' protector. Crate training your puppy is the way to go if you have children, as it defines the dog's territory, and you have a means of giving both the dog and the children time out from each other.

Allowing your children to play with the dog is an excellent way to forge a bond between them, but you should always supervise. This is to prevent the excitement getting out of hand, but also to make sure that games of winning and losing, such as tug-of-war, are not always won by the dog, which will give him delusions of superiority over the child. Managing this sensitive dynamic is key to successful socialization between your dog and your children.

You should always be ready to reprimand your dog if he does behave out of line with your child. Discipline when it is required sets the boundaries, and teaches your dog to respect your child, just as you have taught your child to respect the dog.

When all goes well, which it almost always does with such a friendly breed, growing up with an English Springer Spaniel is one of the greatest gifts you can give your child, and will help them to see the world from a healthy dog's-eye perspective.

# Reactive Dogs

Although English Springer Spaniels are sociable dogs by nature, they are also highly sensitive. This means that some puppies may simply be wired differently from birth, and be predisposed to being highly reactive, or others may be poorly socialized, untrained, or even cruelly treated, resulting in reactive behavior.

Reactive dogs may show aggression toward children, or sometimes a specific gender such as men. This behavior is hard to rehabilitate and can often only be managed by appropriate rehoming. Other dogs may be reactive to cats. Cats are a common nemesis in the minds of any dog, but to a prey-driven Springer Spaniel, they are especially necessary to chase. On the other hand, a puppy brought up with cats will usually achieve a peaceful co-existence with the enemy, and maybe even a reluctant friendship.

It is in your Springer Spaniel's DNA to hunt birds and small furry animals, so if you have chickens or rabbits, you will need to be very careful in the initial stages of introducing your new dog, as his prey drive knows no distinction between what he is allowed to chase and kill, and what is a valued member of his new family. Most Springer Spaniels, however, will learn to respect family pets in time. Chickens usually put them on the right track very quickly as they are directly descended from dinosaurs, and put this quality to effective use in defending themselves. A dog from working lines, however, may be less readily deterred, and keeping your pets separated from your dog by a secure enclosure may be the only answer.

In rare cases, some Springer Spaniels may experience rage syndrome, which is a condition associated with only a small number of breeds, commonly Spaniels. When this occurs, the lights go out behind the dog's eyes as he suddenly becomes reactive. After a short burst of aggression, he is back in the room as if nothing has happened. This condition can be inherited, and registered breeders will not knowingly breed from dogs with rage syndrome. However, if you find that you have a dog with this condition, you may have to consider rehoming through a responsible rescue if you have children, as there is no cure, and the dog can only be managed appropriately throughout its life.

# When Socialization Goes Bad

The good news is, socialization is usually a breeze with an English Springer Spaniel. However, for many of the reasons already outlined, things may occasionally go wrong. This may be because:

- a dog from working lines was purchased as a family dog;

- the dog has an inherited condition such as rage syndrome or is simply highly reactive;

- the dog has not experienced continuity of socialization since leaving the litter;

- the dog has experienced neglect or cruelty in his past;

- the dog has a bad experience, e.g. is attacked by another dog or mishandled by a child.

Owners who find they have taken on more than they can handle should never be afraid to seek professional help. If you have purchased a puppy, there is no disgrace in going back to the breeder to discuss the problems you are experiencing. If there is a genetic element involved, he will be in the best place to advise you on how you might address the issue. In the worst-case scenario, a responsible breeder will take the dog back. It may be that a dog that cannot settle into family life has a vocation elsewhere, such as hunting or in search and rescue.

If you have adopted a rescue dog, and despite assessment, you find yourself out of your depth, you should always contact the rescue for help. Most organizations work with professional behaviorists, who will help you work through the problems if this is a viable option. Otherwise, all rescue dogs come with Rescue Back Up (RBU), which means they can only be re-homed through the original rescue that commits to them for life. There is no shame in accepting things have not worked out if you have given it your best efforts. The dog may go on to thrive in a different environment.

Socializing your English Springer Spaniel should be an enjoyable part of introducing him to his new world, and usually it is problem-free, especially with a bit of foresight. However, if problems arise, they may usually be resolved or at least managed, and you should never be afraid to seek professional help. A well-socialized dog is not only a pleasure to share your life with, he is a happier dog, knowing where he fits into his loving family.

Photo Courtesy of
Billy McKechnie

## CHAPTER 9
# Obedience Training

*"Owner beware, their intelligence can prove to be a problem. They go through stages where they will challenge your ranking. I always tell owners, please prove to me that you are smarter than the dog."*

**Judy Ann Manley**
*Vistah Kennels*

Whether you are bringing an English Springer Spaniel into your home to live as a family member, or you intend to work your dog, it is vitally important that he is obedient. Obedience is deference toward you, his master, and in teaching your dog to live by your rules he will be a calmer and happier dog because he knows that you are in control and he has nothing to worry about. Obedience does not mean that your dog has been dominated into submission, but that he does the things you require of him because he wants to please you. Springer Spaniels, as has been noted already, are very sensitive, form a very close bond with their human, and really crave approval. They are also highly intelligent and communicative, so obedience training is already off to the right start.

If you have been attending puppy classes with your Springer Spaniel, you may find that obedience classes follow on directly once your dog is ready to start learning a few commands. Otherwise, it is worth inquiring at your veterinary practice for the location and contact details of classes in your area. Even if you have trained a dog before, it is worth enrolling in classes, because you have camaraderie and support. It is more fun than training on your own, it becomes

**FUN FACT**

First English Springer Spaniel Best in Show

First English Springer Spaniel Best in Show Between 1907 and 2019, six English Springer Spaniels have been named Best in Show by the Westminster Kennel Club. The first English Springer Spaniel to earn this title was in 1963. His name was CH. Wakefield's Black Knight. He was owned by Mrs. W.J.S. Borie and judged by Mr. Virgil D. Johnson.

a regular discipline, and you may make friends to go on walks together with your dogs. It is beneficial for your dog to continue his socialization, and the distractions of training in an environment with other people and dogs provide just the right element of challenge your clever Springer needs to train him to focus.

There are different training methods when teaching obedience to dogs, so you should check that the class offers a method that you are happy with. Harsh training has fallen out of favor in modern times, and is very unsuited to Springer Spaniels because they are so sensitive. So if you are told to bring a choke chain, you should look for another class. You may be told to bring a clicker, and this can be a very useful training method to reinforce positive training methods. With clicker training, you click and treat when the dog does the right thing. Other positive reinforcement training classes will not require the clicker, but will just require you to bring some irresistible treats such as small pieces of sausage, dried liver chips, or small training treats.

You will also need a short lead, and to be sure your dog is wearing a collar. A waist bag or fanny pack can be useful to keep your training treats to hand, or at least, clothing with pockets.

Positive reinforcement is merely a training method, and there will be many different ways of teaching the basic commands. If you are going to obedience training classes, you should stick to the methods you are being taught, as being consistent is very important. But if it is not possible for you to attend classes, you can use the methods that follow to teach the basics of sit, stay, lie down, and walk on the lead.

# How to Teach Sit

"Sit" is a vital command for your dog's own safety in certain situations, and since it is easy to teach it is a simple first step in the journey of communication with your dog.

To teach "Sit," you need to start by getting your dog's attention fully on you. Your English Springer Spaniel may or may not find this a challenge, as some dogs, especially when they are young puppies, are especially hyperactive and easily distracted, so it is helpful to begin simply by rewarding the dog for making eye contact with the "Look at me" command. Treat the dog when he gives you his attention. If you are clicker-training, you should click then treat.

So with your dog focused on you (which will be easier now that he knows you have treats), move your hand containing the treat up and over his head. His hind quarters will instinctively lower. (If he spins around, set him right and repeat until he lowers his hind quarters correctly.) When his bottom is fully on the floor, give your dog the treat and praise him.

Do not use any command word at this stage, but continue the action over several repetitions until the dog understands that he is being rewarded for lowering his hind quarters to the floor. Once this action is reliably in place, you can use the word "Sit" as you do the hand motion. This way the word becomes associated with the action to your dog.

The next stage is to wean your dog off the hand gesture to just the word. With further repetitions, you can make the hand gesture smaller, until you are using no hand signal or body language, but just the word "Sit." Rewarding each repetition continues to be important to tell your dog that he is doing the right thing.

By this stage, your Springer Spaniel is beginning to feel rather pleased with himself, and is enjoying earning your approval, so it is time to wean him off the treat and onto praise alone. So as you continue the command, do not treat on every repetition. You can still praise your dog, but just produce the treat on intermittent repetitions.

You do not have to reach all these stages in one training session. Keep sessions short for your dog and end on a positive note. Build training into his daily routine so it soon becomes second nature, and it will not be a chore for either of you!

# How to Teach Stay

Your English Springer Spaniel is a lively dog with a short attention span, so the next trick he needs to learn is to stay in the sit position until you release him from it. Here, his intelligence and eagerness to please are in conflict with his puppy hyperactivity, so you will need to keep the session positive by only asking for a very short period in stay to begin with, as you need to set your puppy achievable targets so that he remains encouraged.

Stay should be taught as two commands, "Stay" and "Free." "Free" signifies to the dog that the command period is over. It is also the point at which he has achieved what was asked of him, and he can receive the treat or praise.

Ask your dog for the "Sit" position, and tell him he is a good boy. Make sure he is totally focused on you, and reliably staying in position, and you may use the "Stay" command. Do not use the word "Stay" if your dog is not staying, as he needs to learn to associate the word with the correct action. Keep the treat in your closed hand near to his nose, and he is likely to remain focused. Then after a few seconds, lead your dog away from the sit with the hand containing the treat. As your dog gets up, say "Free" and give him the treat he has waited so patiently for.

With further repetitions, increase the time you ask your dog to stay. When he seems to be staying consistently until released, move away from him while he is in the "Stay." If he follows you before being released, lead him back to the original spot and put him in sit again. Only treat your dog when he gets it right, but as before, always end on a positive note. If you push your dog too quickly, you may find yourself striving too hard for that positive note, whereas if you just progress gradually, your dog will succeed consistently, and this solid improvement will encourage you both.

# How to Teach Lie Down

It is easiest to start teaching the lie down command from a sit position, so you should ask your dog to sit, and reward him to focus his attention on you.

Kneel in front of your dog so that you have good eye contact and bring a treat to his nose, then lower the treat in your closed hand to the floor between his legs, close to his body. Your dog should instinctively lower his front legs, but you should not reward him until both elbows are firmly on the floor. His hind quarters should also go down, but if they do not, you should not push them, which creates resistance, rather you should use your other arm like a limbo pole. Place it across the dog's back, and move the treat forward, so in creeping forward toward the treat, the dog has to lower his back beneath your other arm.

Repeat this exercise several times in succession until it leads to an automatic response. If your dog is struggling, however, don't let him be discouraged—you can teach the command incrementally, rewarding a dip of the head, then a lowering of the elbows, until your dog achieves the full lie down position.

Again, you should not use the command "Lie Down" until your dog is reliably being guided into the correct position with the treat.

Once you have achieved the lie down position with you kneeling in front of your dog, you should raise your body to a crouch and then a stand which will add to the challenge, as you will not be bringing the treat all the way to the floor for his nose to follow.

Photo Courtesy of Charles Phillips

The next step is to wean him off the treat so that he acts consistently on the word alone. So do not reward on every repetition, but vary the times he gets a treat or just some fuss.

Adding "Stay" to the lie down command is the next step, so that you have a dog that will lie down and stay down, which can be extremely useful on many occasions. Just as with stay, you should release your dog from the position with the word "Free." Initially, release him after only a few seconds, building up the time he remains in the lie down position. Remember that staying in one position is challenging for a Springer Spaniel, so as before, set achievable targets, progress slowly, and always end on a positive note!

# How to Teach Walk on the Leash

Your English Springer Spaniel is naturally inclined to walk off-leash, and as previously explained in Chapter 7, solid recall is of paramount importance to enable your Springer to enjoy his freedom. However, all dogs also need to know how to walk nicely on the leash. This can be the hardest of the basic commands to teach your Springer Spaniel, because they are so energetic and they tend to pull hard in their enthusiasm to get wherever they think they are going. However, this is not only exhausting for the owner, it is damaging for the dog. Harnesses may divert the strain from the neck, and control headcollars may make pulling uncomfortable, but they are not the answer. Your Springer Spaniel needs to learn from the outset how to walk nicely by your side on a loose leash. He will not always be a small puppy, and his strength will grow with his size, so you do not want him to think he can use it to get what he wants.

You need to have realistic expectations about walks when training your dog to walk on the leash. This is because you will not be going consistently in one direction or at one speed. You will also have to work to keep your dog's full attention, by being more exciting than his surroundings. To your dog, the leash prevents him from going where he wants, so he will instinctively pull. He needs to disassociate pulling with getting where he wants, and associate going forward with the feel of a loose leash. So every time he pulls, you need to stop. Put your dog in the sit so that you can regain a

Photo Courtesy of
Claudia Bruhn

loose leash, then proceed. Your walk is going to be a continual sequence of stopping and starting in the early stages, and you should also keep changing direction to keep your dog interested. Eventually, he will realize there is a lot more walking and a lot less stopping and sitting when the leash is loose, and he will learn that the right place to be is by your side. Keep your training treats to hand so you can reward his correct behavior when he is walking nicely.

If you are attending puppy classes, you may find your Springer Spaniel puppy learns very quickly in class and walks beautifully on the leash. Likewise if you have started training your dog in the yard. However, once you are outside on a walk, he is a maniac. This is hardly surprising, as there are so many more distractions outdoors and a greater sense of going somewhere. You already know he can do it in class or in the yard, so that is a solid start, but you will find you have to work that bit harder to maintain his attention outside. It may feel frustrating when you just want a nice stroll in the park with your dog, but this time will come. The early months are for training which is a different experience altogether, but a totally worthwhile investment for the years to come.

# Agility and Flyball

English Springer Spaniels can get on very well with Agility because they are so intelligent and athletic. If you have a high energy dog, Agility can help in managing his hyperactivity, and provide a fun pastime that will keep you both in good shape.

Young puppies cannot participate in Agility because of the risk of damaging their growing bones and growth plates. However, by concentrating on obedience training in the first year, your dog is learning to focus on you as his master, to understand about following commands and the principles of reward training. This means that by twelve months when he can start Agility, the basics are already in place.

Agility involves taking your dog around an obstacle course against the clock, and is graded so that initially your dog will only be jumping very low poles. He will also learn the other elements of the course, such as the tunnel, hoops, the A-frame, the walkway, the see-saw and the weaves. As his bones and joints reach maturity, the course becomes more demanding and the jumps will go up. Many Springer Spaniels will love the challenge and exercise involved in Agility and it will increase your bond. However, some Springers may be stressed by the experience, as they can be a sensitive and neurotic breed. Agility should be fun for your dog, so if he does not seem to be enjoying it, you may need to accept that his personality is different and look instead for what he really enjoys.

Flyball is another exciting pastime that your energetic Springer Spaniel may enjoy, as it involves retrieving a ball from the end of an obstacle course and returning with it, and naturally, retrieving is your dog's greatest skill!

If you are less mobile and would find running an Agility course with your dog problematic, Flyball may be a more attractive option, as for the most part, the dog is going it alone.

Photo Courtesy of Lise Sallaup

As with Agility, your dog needs to be twelve months before starting Flyball to ensure his growth plates are closed, but the initial stages will only involve low jumps. Your dog should have good recall, because he will be sent away down the course to retrieve the ball before returning, but beginners' runs are usually fenced each side.

In your dog's first year before he can start Flyball, your recall and obedience training are providing a sure foundation. Fitness and diet are also very important for a dog that is going to take part in high energy activities such as Agility and Flyball.

English Springer Spaniels are a pleasure to train because of their special connection with humans. They want to please, to use their brain, and to be told that they are clever. By always keeping your dog's goals achievable and working within his attention span, you will see him progress in his learning and in the way you communicate with one another. This way, all the while you are bringing the best out in your dog, you are forging a special bond that will last a lifetime, and make for many happy years ahead.

*Photo Courtesy of
Megan Wharrie*

# CHAPTER 10
# Traveling

Whether you plan to travel with your Springer Spaniel when you are going for a walk, going on vacation, or going to the vet, there will surely be some moment in time when you have to travel with your Springer in the car. Some Springers travel excellently in the car, while others are overexuberant and let you know all about it! This might be through barking, jumping around in the car, or whining all the way to your destination. Traveling can be exciting, especially if your Springer associates it with walkies-time, and in this chapter, you will learn plenty of methods to ensure your trip is as uneventful as possible.

## Preparations for Travel

If you do not frequently travel your Springer in a car, it is worth spending some time getting him used to it. Some dogs find traveling in the car stressful. This leads to drooling and nausea, which eventually leads to anxiety when being placed in the car. To accustom your dog to car travel, start by allowing him some time in the area of the car in which he will travel.

Make this a fun experience. For example, play with his favorite toy or give him his dinner there.

## HELPFUL TIP

### Comfort at the Kennel

If you choose to board your dog at the kennel, there are a few things you can do to make his time more comfortable while you're away. Consider bringing your dog's bed or bedding to the kennel, as well as an item of clothing you've worn next to your skin so that your dog has a familiar scent in his new environment. It's also a good idea to provide the kennel with enough of the food that your dog is accustomed to eating to last the duration of your trip. Some kennels also offer additional exercise and socialization, as well as grooming for your dog, by request.

Before you set off on your travels, whether it be to the local park for a walk or far away on vacation, there are some vital preparations you must make. Your dog will be away from home, so having him microchipped and wearing an identification tag on his collar will ensure he is easily returned to you, should he escape. Make sure his microchip details are up to date though, as they are useless if your cell number is incorrect. The identification tag should have your contact number on. Some people also like to include their address. Traditionally, the name of your dog should also be included; however, this can cause issues if your dog is stolen, as a thief can then prove they know the name that your dog responds to.

If you are traveling far away, taking your dog to the vet for a health check may be required. At this appointment, you can collect any chronic medication which your dog may need while traveling, as well as any flea or worming treatments which may be due. You can also ensure your dog's vaccines are up to date. He may require boosters or additional vaccines or tests, such as rabies, depending on the area you are traveling to. If you are going abroad, your vet will be able to give a letter stating fitness to travel by plane, as well as advise and complete passport and export paperwork for you.

Before you leave your vet practice, check that you have their number preprogrammed into your phone, so that if your Springer has to visit a vet while you are out of town, you can quickly provide the details of your regular vet so that they can exchange medical histories, if relevant. It is also useful to do your research, and investigate which is the closest veterinary practice to where you are staying. Preprogram this number into your cell too, as then if you need it while you are away, you will not waste time searching for a local vet practice and their details.

# Traveling in a Car

It is your choice where in your car you choose to transport your Springer; however, if you have a particularly exuberant Spaniel, you may want to consider some form of restraint. It will be dangerous if your Springer decides to climb forward to be with you in the front.

Photo Courtesy of Andrew MacVicar

Many owners choose to transport their Springer in a crate. These can fit on the back seat or in the hatch if you have a large car. A crate should be large enough for your dog to stand up, stretch, turn around, and sit down comfortably without touching the sides. It should be made of strong material and not have any sharp or jutting edges where your dog can injure themselves. Each side should be ventilated and it should be placed in a position in your car where air can easily flow through it.

A crate can be advantageous to intense dogs, as if you also use it in the house, it will become their area of safety and calm. Therefore, if you have an anxious or excited Spaniel, it will help keep them calm in the car. It will also ensure it is impossible for them to jump over the seats to join you in the front.

Some people choose to transport their dog loose in the hatch of the car instead. This is an easy option if you have a large car; however, if you choose to do this, it is advisable to purchase a dog guard which fits behind the back seats to stop your Springer from jumping over. It is worth considering that this area of the car will then become hairy and dirty from your dog, so if you wish to keep a clean car you may consider tailored hatch bags or liners.

The safest method of traveling with your dog in a car is by purchasing a dog harness with a seatbelt attachment. Your dog will sit on the back seat of the car and be attached to the seatbelt, which not only will ensure he is safe in a crash, but also will stop him from moving around in the car. If you choose this option, you may wish to cover your seats with a seat cover or a dog bed to stop them from becoming dirty for the next person to sit in the back of your car.

Dogs have the ability to become motion sick as well as humans. Therefore, if you notice him smacking his lips or drooling excessively, this might be the cause. Your veterinarian can provide travel sickness pills for you to give him half an hour before you travel. Also, transporting him on an empty stomach will help prevent his nausea.

When you travel for long distances, ensure everything you need is within easy reach. These things include a leash, water, and food. You should offer your dog food at least every 12 hours, and water at least every 4 hours. Your dog should also be given ample opportunity to relieve himself and burn off some energy. If you need to stop to go to a shop or fill up with fuel, remember, dogs die in hot cars very easily. This can be prevented by ensuring a window is open, you are parked in the shade, and there is plenty of fresh airflow to where your dog is sitting.

*Photo Courtesy of Louise Stewart*

# Traveling by Plane

When you are traveling abroad, some airlines will allow you to bring your dog as long as they are over 12 weeks old. A small English Springer Spaniel may be small enough to travel in the cabin with you; however, most airlines will probably enforce them travelling in the hold. The exception to this is if your Springer is a service dog. In that case, they can travel with their handler at all times.

If your dog must travel in the hold, he will need to travel within an airline-approved crate. Each airline has different requirements, and it is your responsibility to check that you have everything in place for when your dog flies.

Most airlines require you to present a certificate of health from your veterinarian to prove that your dog is fit to fly. This is usually in addition to a passport, vaccination history, and export paperwork, depending on your destination. Your veterinarian will be able to advise you on what you need.

Before you travel, it is important to research the forecasted temperatures at that time of year. If it is below 45 degrees Fahrenheit or above 85 degrees Fahrenheit during departure, arrival, and during connections, your dog may be refused travel. This is unless you can provide a letter from your veterinarian confirming your dog is frequently subjected to these temperatures, and therefore is used to them.

# Vacation Lodging

Before you book a vacation, check if you are allowed to bring your dog. If you are lucky enough to be allowed to bring your dog with you, you must remember not everyone who visits that accommodation will like dogs. Start by asking the receptionist where you can walk your dog to relieve himself, and always pick up his poop after him. Try to stop him from barking by not leaving him alone in this strange place. This will also prevent him from chewing on furniture if he is naturally anxious. If he is crate-trained and you have brought his crate, he will have the advantage of a familiar, safe place where he will feel more at home, and you can relax knowing he is not causing any damage.

When you leave the accommodation, try to leave it in the same state that you found it. Your hosts should not need to do more than clean the room to make it appear that there was never a dog there.

# Leaving Your Dog at Home

If you choose to leave your Springer at home, rather than take him on vacation, you have several options regarding his care. Some options will suit certain dogs better than others, and only you can judge which is best for your dog.

The first option is to book him to stay at a boarding kennel. These are establishments which are professionally run. The staff at boarding kennels are usually very familiar with all types of dogs, their care, and managing ailments. Your dog is most likely to stay in a kennel which has two sections to it; an indoor or sheltered bed area, and an outdoor run for stretching his legs and doing his business. Once or twice a day, your dog will be taken out for a walk by the staff or let out into a large communal area to play. If your Springer is easygoing, this may be a good option for him; however, for most Springers, they will require more one-on-one attention than a kennel can provide.

The next option is to ask a friend, family member, or the original breeder of your dog to look after him. This is usually in their own home. This is an

excellent option for your Springer if he likes plenty of attention, as he will get one-on-one time with another person. Also, you know who is looking after him and can vouch for their responsibility. If they have their own dog, make sure prior to making arrangements that they get on with your Springer. While your dog might be pleased to have a dog to play with, the other dog may be less pleased about the new addition to their household. Reciprocal arrangements can work very well with dog-owning friends or family members, so you can look after each other's dogs when you take a vacation away from home. For the dogs, this is also a good arrangement as they become familiar with the carer, their dog, and their home.

Finally, if you wish for your dog to have plenty of attention, yet for them to stay in a familiar environment, you may find that a house sitter is the best option for you. These are professionals who come and live in your home while you are away, to look after your dog. Not only is this a great option for your dog, but it also keeps your house safe. If you decide this is the best option for you and your dog, meeting up with the house sitter on neutral territory, such as a dog walk, will be a good opportunity for you all to get to know each other.

Springers are sensitive dogs to change, and therefore only you will know what is best for your Springer; whether to travel with him or leave him behind. But whatever you choose to do, holidays should be enjoyed by all, so take time to plan them well and then you will be able to enjoy your travels to the full extent.

# CHAPTER 11
# Nutrition

Springers seem to fall into one of two categories when it comes to food: picky, delicate eaters or ravenous, greedy dogs. Regardless of how your Springer eats, nutrition plays an important role in his health. A healthy diet will lead to a healthy dog. But there is so much choice in the pet store. This chapter will teach you all about nutrition and what to look out for in a quality food.

## Importance of Nutrition

Health and nutrition are closely intertwined. To ensure your dog is healthy, he must eat, and successfully absorb carbohydrates, fat, proteins, minerals, vitamins, and fiber. If any part of the digestive system is not functioning well, it will affect the body's ability to absorb certain nutrients. Diets can aid in improving the health of these dogs, as the quantities of each nutrient can be adjusted to ensure they are receiving the correct amounts to allow the body to function optimally.

Diets also affect the body in the opposite way. If a poor-quality diet has the wrong quantities of nutrients, then it will have a negative impact on health. For example, if a puppy is fed a diet with too little calcium and phosphorus, his bones will not grow appropriately, or if an elderly dog is fed a diet high in sodium, it will cause the kidneys to work harder than they need to. Therefore, it is imperative that you feed your Springer a quality, balanced diet, appropriate for his age and energy levels. Springers are naturally energetic, and therefore most will benefit from a slightly higher calorie diet than a normal dog food. This is especially the case if you own a working Springer.

**HELPFUL TIP**
**Choosing the Right Formula**

Once you've decided on the best brand of food for your dog, make sure to purchase the correct formula based on your dog's weight and age. Most brands provide a variety of products to meet the needs of puppies, small breeds, large breeds, and senior dogs. For more information about choosing the right food for your dog, talk to your local veterinarian.

Springer Spaniels also benefit from diets which are high in omega-3 and omega-6 fatty acids. These are found in oily foods such as fish and seeds. They are excellent at maintaining the luscious coat of your Springer, as well as keeping his very active joints well lubricated. If you have an older Springer with arthritis, which will be discussed further in Chapter 18, omega fatty acids will also reduce the inflammation in his sore joints.

# Commercial Food

When you first bring home your new Springer Spaniel puppy, it is best to initially continue the food the breeder has been giving, as long as it is a commercial puppy food. The stress of moving home can upset the sensitive stomach of a puppy, and changing the food to a new rich diet is likely to upset it even further. Therefore, to avoid causing diarrhea, allow your puppy to settle for a week, then slowly change over to your new food, over the course of a couple of weeks.

Choosing a new food for your dog can seem daunting. The pet store, vet clinic, supermarket, and internet, between them, offer you hundreds of options. You must first decide whether you wish your Springer to eat dry or wet food, or a mixture of both. Dry food provides concentrated ingredients, so you will need less volume, compared to wet food, to provide your dog with the same number of calories. Dry food also helps to keep teeth healthy, as when your dog bites through the kibble, it will provide friction against the teeth. This means less tartar will build up in the mouth.

Wet food, however, will have fewer starchy filler ingredients, which means it is closer to the natural food a dog would have eaten in the wild.

Photo Courtesy of
Billy McKechnie

It also means it will not swell in the stomach, like dry food. Swelling food can be a problem as it can make your Springer feel like he needs the toilet urgently. Wet food is also significantly more palatable, so for Springers who are picky, wet food might be the answer.

After deciding whether to feed dry food, wet food, or a mixture, you must choose the life-stage. Puppies should always be fed a puppy or junior food. These foods are higher in protein, calcium, and phosphorus, which are important for growing bodies. When your puppy reaches full size, which is usually between 9 and 18 months, he can slowly be moved onto an adult food over the course of a couple of weeks. Adult food can have several forms: normal, active, sensitive, breed specific, etc. Springers are usually best suited to either normal or active diets, depending on your dog's energy levels. For later in life, there are diet options which are for specific ailments, such as kidney disease or liver disease, as well as senior foods, which will be discussed further in Chapter 18.

If you are not sure about which food to choose, you can ask your local pet store consultant, vet, or veterinary nurse. All these people will have had training about the diets they sell and are useful sources of information. Rest assured though, whatever food you choose, if it is on the shelf, it must have met AAFCO standards.

# BARF and Homemade Diets

Bones and raw food (BARF) and homemade diets are becoming increasingly popular in the canine world, especially amongst working dog homes. The idea behind them is that you know exactly what you are feeding your dog and can source it locally and know that it is non-GMO. Also, the food can be made up of quality ingredients and not full of bulking ingredients. The difference between BARF and homemade diets is that BARF diets contain raw meat and uncooked bones, while homemade diets consist of cooked meats and no bones.

The benefit of BARF diets in particular is that they are very similar to what dogs would have eaten in the wild. BARF and homemade diets both come with considerable risks though. Most owners do not consult a veterinary nutritionist when first deciding the recipes for their dogs. As a result, the recipes are often imbalanced, which can lead to stunted growth, weak bones and bladder stones. In addition, BARF diets bring with them considerable health and safety risks. Raw food can contain organisms such as Salmonella and E.coli, which can cause major illnesses in vulnerable people. Therefore, if you have elderly people or children in your house, you should advise them not to touch your dog if he is on a BARF diet because bacteria may be transferred to the coat via the dog's saliva when he grooms himself. The raw bones are also a concern in a barf diet. In theory, they should be able to be digested by the stomach acid; however, unfortunately this is frequently not the case, and therefore your dog may be at higher risk for perforations or blockages from these bones.

# Pet Food Labels

All pet food labels must follow set guidelines, if they comply with AAFCO standards. The first thing to look at on a pet food label is the ingredients list. Ingredients are listed in order of quantity. Therefore, if chicken is first on the list, this will be the main ingredient. A quality food should have a meat-based protein as the first ingredient. However, it is worth noting that ground-up dried meat, known as meal, contains 300% more protein than its fresh counterpart per gram, and therefore can be much further down the list in weight, yet contribute the same, if not more, protein than the ingredient at the top of the list.

There are many potential ingredients in dog food. Meats make up the majority of the protein content, and can be derived from chicken, beef, turkey, lamb, fish, venison, and duck. These proteins can be pure meat or meat-derivatives, but the label must state the source. Some meats are more allergenic than others, and therefore if your Springer suffers with itchy skin, venison and duck are better than common meats, such as chicken or beef.

Fish proteins are excellent sources of omega-3 and omega-6, which, as discussed earlier, contribute to healthy joints, skin, and coat.

In addition to meat ingredients, there are usually many different types of grains, vegetables, and sometimes fruits. Grains can make some dogs gassy, and anecdotally, can cause skin reactions. Therefore, they may not be suited to all dogs; however, if your dog does not react to grains, they can be excellent sources of dietary fiber to keep your dog regular. Vegetables and fruits are ingredients which contribute most of the minerals and vitamins to the diet. You will most

Photo Courtesy of Charles Phillips

commonly see potatoes, sweet potatoes, peas, and carrots listed on the ingredients list. These are all excellent sources of vitamins A, B, and C, as well as magnesium, potassium, and iron. In combination, this will help keep the eyes and brain healthy, keep the heart beating in a regular rhythm, boost the immune system, improve the production of red blood cells, and aid in nerve conduction.

Also on the label is the "Guaranteed Analysis." This details the percentage of carbohydrates, proteins, fat, fiber, ash, and moisture in the diet. These details are per gram of ready-to-eat food, and therefore cannot be directly compared without first doing some calculations.

For example, if a wet food is 75% wet, then it means the dry content is 25%. If the protein level is then 5%, this can be converted by dividing by the dry matter percentage: 5/0.25 = 20% protein on a dry matter basis. Then if a similar dry food, which you wanted to compare, had a moisture content of 10% and a dry content of 90%, with a protein level of 20%, the calculation would be as follows: 20/0.9 = 22.2% protein on a dry matter basis.

In conjunction with the ingredients, once you have adjusted the guaranteed analysis, it is a great tool to analyze the food.

# Weight Monitoring

If you are struggling to keep your Springer at an appropriate weight, you should seek the advice of your veterinarian or veterinary nurse. They will be able to advise what would be the most appropriate weight of your dog. Often, it is as simple as feeding the recommended requirements on the packaging for the target weight, rather than the actual weight of your dog, which will help adjust his weight. However, if this does not work, you can increase or decrease the food intake by 10%, and gradually assess his weight change on a monthly basis.

The best way to monitor weight, though, is not through figures, but instead, body condition scores. An ideal body condition score is 4 to 5, and the range goes from 1 (emaciated) to 9 (obese). The scores are standardized for anybody to use, and are easy and repeatable from dog to dog. Springers will require hands-on assessing, as their luscious long fur may obscure the outline of the ribs, waist, and abdominal tuck. These are the descriptions of the following scores:

**BCS 1 = Emaciated.** Ribs, lumbar vertebral projections, and bony prominences around the pelvis are clearly visible. There is severe loss of muscle and no body fat.

**BCS 3 = Underweight.** Ribs can be felt with ease and might be visible. Not much fat present. The abdomen tucks up at the flank and a waist can be seen from the top. Some bony projections can be seen. Easy to see top of lumbar vertebrae.

**BCS 5 = Ideal.** Minimal fat over the ribs and can easily feel them. Waist and ribs are visible when standing above the dog. Tucked abdomen when viewed from the side.

**BCS 7 = Overweight.** Fat present over ribs and need some pressure to feel them. Fat deposits over rump and around tail base. Cannot easily view waist. Abdominal tuck present but slight.

**BCS 9 = Obese.** Lots of fat around the base of tail, spine and chest. Abdomen may bulge behind the ribs. No waist or abdominal tuck. Fat deposits on neck and limbs.

For many Springer Spaniel owners, weight can become a constant battle. You may have a picky eater with boundless energy, and putting on weight seems impossible. Alternatively, you may have a Springer who will eat the bowl that the food is put in, if given the chance, and keeping the weight off is a constant challenge. However, with the advice of your veterinarian or veterinary nurse, you will certainly be able to find a quality food which will help you with your battles, and ensure your Springer is as healthy as can be.

*Photo Courtesy of Jennifer Rairigh*

# CHAPTER 12
# Dental Care

Just as we must clean our teeth on a daily basis, it is important also to care for your Springer Spaniel's teeth to avoid dental issues as your dog ages. In this chapter we will look at dental hygiene, the dental conditions your Springer might suffer from, and the procedures available to have a healthy mouth.

# Importance of Dental Care

Many people do not realize that part of a good dog hygiene practice involves looking after your dog's teeth. This is a common misunderstanding, as in the wild, dogs do not clean their teeth, and they are just fine. However, your Springer Spaniel is not a wild dog. Wild ancestors were able to gnaw on bones to keep their teeth clean, whereas the diets that domestic dogs are fed are greatly different.

Without routine dental care, your Springer may end up developing dental disease, which can be painful, smelly, and cause a loss of appetite. It is also not pleasant having your Springer Spaniel cuddled up as close to you as he can get, breathing in your face with rotten-smelling breath. It is easy to prevent dental disease with a daily dental routine, but this must become a habit from a young age to be tolerated well.

# Dental Anatomy

The tooth is a bony structure, comprising of two parts; the crown, which you can see, and the roots, which are under the gum. Some teeth have one root, others two, and some molars have three.

The first teeth to appear are the 28 deciduous (baby) teeth. These gradually fall out in the first year of life to be replaced with 42 adult teeth. The small teeth at the front are called incisors, and next to them are the large, pointed canines. In the wild, these teeth would be used by the dog to grab hold of their prey, as well as nibble pieces of meat off of the bone. Along the cheeks are pre-molars and then at the back, molars. These teeth are larger and flatter, and are used to grind harder food.

## HELPFUL TIP
### It's Never Too Early

Much like hu man dental hygiene, what you do for your dog's teeth at home will make the biggest difference between healthy teeth and a diseased mouth. It's never too early to introduce a toothbrushing routine into your dog's life. Make sure to brush your dog's teeth when he is calm and relaxed instead of agitated. Creating a calm and positive attitude towards dental hygiene at an early age, as well as regularly visiting the vet, can help your dog avoid dental issues later in life.

Each tooth is made up of bone, coated in a protective layer of enamel. In the very center of the tooth is the pulp. This is a fleshy section filled with nerves. If this becomes exposed, it can cause considerable tooth ache.

Surrounding the tooth is the tooth socket. This is the area inside the skull in which the tooth root sits. It is held in place by a very strong ligament all the way around the tooth. This is called the periodontal ligament.

## Tartar Buildup and Gingivitis

Tartar is the buildup of leftover food material and bacteria around the base of the crown. It can cause serious consequences, as the body reacts to the bacteria by sending white blood cells to the area. As a result, the gums surrounding the teeth with tartar on become inflamed and very sore. This is called gingivitis. As the gums become more inflamed, the periodontal ligament slackens, causing the tooth to become wobbly and eventually fall out.

Owners are frequently under the impression that if their dog is eating, they do not have a painful mouth. Many dogs will eat despite their mouths being sore and foul tasting.

Preventing tartar buildup is the key to preventing gingivitis. This is addressed a little later in this chapter. Once tartar has built up, it is difficult to remove without a dental procedure, but with diligent dental care, it can be improved upon.

# Worn Teeth

Springer Spaniels love to be outside, and they also love to pick up sticks and stones to chew on a walk. This is a bad idea on many levels. Not only do they pose a risk to the guts for blockages and penetrations if swallowed, but they are also very bad for the teeth.

Stones in particular will grind down teeth, and a lifetime of chewing inanimate objects will gradually wear down the teeth to expose the pulp. A particularly hard stone may even crack a tooth. Once the pulp is exposed, the bare nerves will be sending pain signals to the brain continuously. Tooth rebuilding is not frequently done in veterinary practice, and therefore tooth extraction is usually the treatment of choice. This can be tricky if there is little crown left for the veterinarian to grab hold of, however, once out, your Springer will be significantly more comfortable.

# Epulis

An epulis is a benign tumor of the mouth. It originates in the gum tissue, often in the region of the canines or incisors. There are three different types of epulis which your Springer might develop:

1. Fibromatous – this is tough tissue made out of fibers.

2. Ossifying – this type contains bone cells as well, and can develop into cancer.

3. Acanthomatous – this is the most dangerous, as when it grows, it destroys the tissue surrounding it, including the bones, but it will not spread to other parts of the body.

It is not known exactly why epulis develop. Some breeds are more prone to developing them, but gum inflammation may play a role as well.

Apart from a lump in the mouth, you might notice foul-smelling breath, a loss of appetite, and blood in the mouth. In extreme cases, it may interfere with breathing. The lump itself will look a lot like gum tissue, and when it is small, it may not easily be distinguished from the gum itself.

Epulis need to be removed with surgery. This is easier if done early in its growth, as a margin of healthy tissue must also be taken otherwise it will regrow. If it is completely removed, the prognosis is good.

# Dental Care

Keeping your dog's teeth clean is important from a young age. Once the health of the mouth has become compromised, saving all the teeth from loss and decay is extremely difficult. Prevention is always better than cure. Teaching your dog to tolerate dental care from a puppy should be done by all new owners. With that being said, starting to care for your dog's teeth from an older age is better than no dental care at all.

## Teeth brushing

Brushing the teeth should be the main preventative measure that all owners should take. This will help keep them clean, stop tartar buildup, and ensure that thorough dental checks are regularly performed. The teeth should always be brushed with a dog toothpaste, as human toothpaste can be toxic to dogs. Dogs also much prefer the meaty flavor of dog toothpaste. The toothpaste formulated for dogs will have enzymes in it which help to dissolve any tartar which has started to build up.

There are several options for brushing tools. Your Springer Spaniel is big enough for a brush, but if you find a rubber finger brush easier, this will also suffice. You should brush your Springer's teeth daily. Start with the incisors at the front, then the canines, then pull the cheeks all the way back to reach the back molars and premolars. You should not expect brushing to be accepted by your dog immediately, so ensure that you make it a fun experience, with plenty of positive reinforcement.

## Dental chews

Dental chews are an easy way of keeping your dog's teeth healthy; however, they are not a replacement for brushing. The idea behind the chews is that they suck off the tartar as the tooth sinks into it. Dental chews contain calories, and therefore it is important to remember that any calories which are given in the form of treats are removed from the daily caloric intake of your Spaniel.

Some owners prefer natural chews for their dog. Traditionally bones were given to dogs to gnaw on, but bones splinter, shatter, and can cause blockages, so they are not recommended treats. An excellent alternative is to offer your dog a piece of deer antler. These are long lasting and excellent at removing tartar, while being completely safe.

## Dental wash

Mouthwash for your dog is becoming increasingly popular in the dog world. It is used with ease, as you simply add it to the water every day. It is important that human mouthwash is never used, as like human toothpaste, it can be toxic and lead to liver damage.

The water with added mouthwash should be completely replaced with fresh water on a daily basis. This will ensure the enzymes in the mouthwash are working efficiently, as well as provide your dog with fresh water. Like with the toothpaste, the enzymes help to dissolve the tartar off the teeth. It is less effective than brushing, however, and if your Springer Spaniel already has considerable tartar buildup, it will probably only prevent it from worsening, rather than treat the problem.

## Dental food

Finally, dental food is available from some of the leading veterinary food manufacturers on the market. These foods are kibbles, with big pieces which require your dog to bite through them before they can be swallowed. The action of biting through the kibble creates an abrasion on the tooth, and therefore removes tartar which is building up. The pieces are usually slightly soft too, so that as your dog bites, a bit of suction is created against the tooth, which aids in the function of the food.

If your Springer Spaniel has excellent teeth, there is no need for him to eat a dental diet. A normal dry food will suffice in preventing tartar build up on the teeth.

Photo Courtesy of Charles Phillips

# Dental Procedures

If your Springer Spaniel is unfortunate enough to have dental disease which requires a dental procedure, this can be done in any general practice vet. Generally, dental procedures are not difficult, and it is a procedure in which a vet has daily experience.

Your dog will need to go into the clinic for the day, but he will usually come home in the afternoon, once he has awoken fully. The procedure requires a general anesthetic, as dental tools can be sharp and therefore if your Springer is wiggling around, which is likely to be the case, this can be dangerous for all involved.

Your vet will start by scaling the teeth to remove all the tartar. This will allow him to see all the teeth at the junction of the gums. After that, he will run a dental probe around this area to investigate whether there are any pockets where the periodontal ligament has become damaged. He will also see if any of the teeth are wobbly. If this is the case, these teeth will need to be removed.

Tooth removal requires loosening of the periodontal ligaments which hold the tooth in place. A tool called an elevator is used to do this. Once loose, gentle traction will pull the tooth out. Some vets will close the tooth socket, and others will keep it open, depending on how large the hole is and how much bacteria is in the mouth.

Even if your Springer has to have some teeth out, he will feel significantly better after the dental procedure. It is likely that he will immediately be happy to eat; however, providing soft food for a few days will help with his comfort levels.

While a dental procedure may seem invasive, your dog's health and welfare will be significantly improved with one. Nevertheless, this can be prevented with diligent care of his mouth from a young age so that your Springer can always have a healthy, pain-free mouth with fresh breath.

# CHAPTER 13
# Grooming

There's nothing better than having your Springer cuddle up to you and place their head, with their long, soft, silky ears, on your lap or against your chest. English Springer Spaniels love to be affectionate, and Springer cuddles are wonderful, but with them comes a load of hair shedding onto your clothes, which you never seem to be able to get rid of. Grooming on a regular basis will ensure you keep on top of loose hair, so that your house and yourself are less covered.

## About the Coat

An English Springer Spaniel coat is either flat or wavy, but in either case it is medium to long in length, with beautiful feathering on the chest, backs of legs, and belly. The coat is a double coat, which means the undercoat ensures they stay dry when working in the field.

The coat can come in a couple of colors; black and white or liver and white. Springers which are bred from working lines typically are whiter with patches of color, sometimes with some ticking, as this allows them to easily be spotted when working in the field. Show spaniels, on the other hand, are generally more color than white.

The working Springers also tend to have a coarser and shorter coat than the show Springers, who have a silky, fine, longer coat.

The coat sheds in the spring and summer months, when the weather is heating up, and they do not need so much of the undercoat.

## Coat Health

*"I keep my dogs short during hunting season to make it easier to remove burrs, etc. from their coats, but there is also strong evidence that a full coat actually better protects the dogs from the elements."*

**Greg Butler**
*Walnut Run Kennels*

*Photo Courtesy of
Marsha Frame*

Photo Courtesy of
Laura Coad

Part of owning an English Springer Spaniel is keeping up with grooming. If you allow your Springer to run through undergrowth and bushes, which he will surely want to do, it will be a regular occurrence that he comes home covered in bush, burrs, tangles, and mats. These can easily be addressed with regular grooming.

Springer owners tend to choose one of three styles when it comes to maintaining their dogs' coat. The first style is the bench style. This is fully natural, where no excessive thinning or trimming has been done to the coat. As a result, the hair on the back and top of the neck may become coarser and wavier than the other styles. This style will require regular upkeep, with brushing every second day, and removing burrs and undergrowth from the hair on a daily basis. The coat will need to be washed down with water after a muddy walk to ensure that none of the areas of feathering become matted, and a shampoo once a month will keep it silky and fresh.

**HELPFUL TIP**
Grooming Safety

Finding the best salon for your dog can be a stressful task. Dog groomers and salons are not regulated by the U.S. government, but the AKC has found a solution to this problem by offering a Safety in the Salon course as part of the AKC S.A.F.E. (Safety, Assurance, Fundamentals, Education) Grooming Program. By completing this course, passing the test, and agreeing to the AKC S.A.F.E. oath, groomers and salons can become AKC S.A.F.E. certified. To search for groomers and salons who are certified as part of this program, visit the AKC Groomerfinder at www.marketplace.akc.org/search-groomers.

The next style which some Springer owners choose is a full clip-out. This requires clipping short the whole coat. Some owners opt for something in between this and the bench style where the feathers and ear hair are still kept, but are cut shorter. This style will require a trip to the groomer every six weeks to maintain, but maintenance in between groomer trips is significantly easier than any other style coat. This style ensures that there are no mats or undergrowth in the coat, and it is kept clean and tidy. It is also easier to spot any ticks, and to prevent fleas. Be aware though, that once totally clipped out, the hair will never regrow exactly how it was. It will usually come through coarser or wavier if left to grow back to its normal length.

Finally, there is the show style. This requires immense effort to maintain, but a show style coat can look impressive. The hair on the face, tops of ears, and neck are all kept short. The base of the neck is then carefully blended into the long feathers of the bib to ensure a seamless transition.

The hair on the back is thinned out and cut shorter, and again it is carefully blended into the longer hair of the undercarriage. The hair of the hindquarters and the tail is cut short so that the physique of the Springer can be seen clearly, and finally the long feathering of the legs is carefully maintained. This type of style requires a lot of patience to get right, and maintenance in between. Not only will your Springer's coat require attention after every walk, but also preventing the ears from dropping in their water or food bowls is important. As mentioned in Chapter 4, you can purchase bowls which are narrower at the top than the bottom to aid your Springer's floppy ears to hang outside the bowl.

# External Parasites

*"Always keep your dog protected from pests. Use a good flea and tick prevention. Be wise and do your homework and study whatever product you decide to use. If you run them in fields, be aware of the dangers of foxtails. They can get into a dogs bloodstream and kill them. Be diligent in going over them once you return from an outing."*

**Judy Ann Manley**
*Vistah Kennels*

When it comes to external parasites, prevention is better than cure. While fleas seem to get all the public attention, lice, mites, and ticks are also important to prevent to ensure your Springer Spaniel is itch free. Fleas and ticks can also carry diseases, transmitted through their bites, and therefore it is paramount to keep on top of preventative treatments.

Fleas live off the dog 90% of the time, and only jump on to your Springer to feed. So, if you notice that your Springer has a flea problem, you should not only treat your dog, but also the environment. This can easily be done with a vacuum, hot wash of bedding, and spray specifically to kill fleas. Treatments must be done for at least three months in a row, as the eggs are not usually killed by the treatments. Therefore, repetitive treatments will swiftly kill off the hatching eggs, before they have a chance to mature into adults.

Ticks are found in areas where wildlife run. They are particularly common in long grasses and woodland areas. If you regularly walk your dogs in these types of areas, a tick prevention collar is a wise idea. If not, you can routinely treat for other external parasites, but just monitor the coat close-ly, and remove ticks if you see them. Ticks may be too small to notice imme-diately after your walk, only swelling to the size of a small bean once they have fed, when they are more easily detected. To remove a tick, you should use a tick twisting fork, not tweezers, as this will ensure the head of the tick is also removed. If left in, it can cause a local infection in the area of the bite.

External parasite treatments can come in a variety of forms. Many peo-ple choose to use a pipette spot on treatment on the back of the neck. How-ever, they can come in the forms of sprays, collars, tablets, and treats, all of varying lengths of duration.

# Nail Clipping

Clipping the nails of your Springer Spaniel should be introduced from a young age. If your Springer puppy is not used to having this done, it can be-come a stressful procedure for your older dog. Since Springers are sensitive in nature, the attention, coupled with the fiddling around, can make them considerably more anxious.

To clip your Springer's nails, you will need a dog nail clipper. These come in a variety of sizes, but a large one is best for a Springer Spaniel. Start by pushing back any long hair in the area, so that you can see the nails very clearly. Check that you are confident you know where the quick is. This is the fleshy middle of the nail, which if you cut it will be extremely sore for your dog, as well as bleed profusely. Try not to panic if this happens, as you will only make your worried Springer even more upset. Just calmly place a wad of cotton wool on the claw, and hold pressure on it for 3-5 minutes. Un-fortunately, with black claws, it is much more difficult to know where to cut, and therefore being conservative is always best.

Where your dog regularly walks will influence how often you must cut his nails. If you walk on concrete or tar on a daily basis, you may find that you rarely need to cut his nails, as they naturally file down. On the other hand, if you always walk where the ground is soft, and your house is main-ly carpeted, then it is likely you will have to clip his nails every 1-2 months.

# Ear Cleaning

*"Owning an ESS can be a challenge to keep healthy ear canals. It is a closed environment which harbours bacteria. An ESS owner needs to learn how to keep the ear canal clean and dry."*

**Judy Ann Manley**
*Vistah Kennels*

Springers have incredible ears. But that beauty comes with a cost. Floppy ears regularly become damp and warm, and are a perfect breeding ground for bacteria and yeast. This is worsened if your Springer is a keen swimmer and regularly gets them wet. With the breed seeming to have a magnetic affinity to water, it is very important that you make ear cleaning part of your regular routine.

Ear cleaner can be bought from the pet store, internet, or vet; however, the vet will provide you with one which is perfect for the health of your dog's ears. Ear cleaner helps to dissolve wax and dirt which has made its way into the ear, as well as changing the pH to reduce the chances of ear infections, and helps dry the ear out.

You should start by holding up the flap of the ear, then placing the nozzle into the ear canal and giving a squirt. When you have put a sufficient amount in, place the ear flap back down, and massage the whole area for 20-30 seconds. He will then likely shake his head when you let go, but this is a good thing, as it brings all the loosened wax and dirt to the surface. You can wipe this away with some cotton wool. Then repeat with the other ear.

Ear cleaning should be done after every swim, as well as once a month if you have a Springer who does not have ear problems. However, if your dog has recurrent infections or smelly, waxy ears, cleaning the ears every 1-2 weeks, or as directed by your vet, will help maintain a healthy environment in the ear canals.

# Anal Glands

The anal glands sit at a four and eight o'clock position on the inside of the anus. They are redundant sacs which can easily fill up with fecal material if your Springer's stools are looser than usual. A quality diet will usually ensure that the stools are normal, but if you find he struggles, fiber supplements in the diet can help firm up the stools to provide more stimulation as the stools pass.

When the anal sacs become filled, they will need to be emptied by a vet, veterinary nurse, or groomer to ensure they do not become infected. It is easy to tell if they are full because your Springer will definitely let you know. He will rub his bottom along the ground, known as scooting, to try to relieve the discomfort of the filled sacs. He is also likely to lick the area, possibly obsessively, as Springers tend to become obsessed when something is bothering them. If you miss those clues, you certainly won't miss the repugnant fishy odor that filled anal glands bring into your house!

If your dog has recurrent issues with his anal glands, they can be removed, but that can be a risky procedure as the nerves to the anal sphincter run just behind them. If damaged, the anal sphincter can become leaky, which not only is unhygienic for your dog and the house, but unenjoyable for everyone. Before surgery, your vet may try routine emptying every two weeks, or flushing them under anesthetic.

Keeping up with your Springer Spaniel's looks will require more effort than the average breed of dog, but by following the advice in this chapter, he will both look and feel great, and you will have a striking and handsome dog.

# CHAPTER 14
# Preventative Veterinary Medicine

Preventing ill health is always better than cure. Therefore, by keeping up to date with preventative veterinary treatment, you can ensure your English Springer Spaniel has the best opportunity to be in top condition. This chapter will outline all the preventative veterinary treatments which you should consider for your dog.

## Choosing a Veterinarian

Your relationship with your veterinarian should be like your relationship with a hairdresser. Once you have found one you like, you stick with them long term, as they know you, they know your dog, and they know your dog's problems and personality. But finding a veterinarian when you have a new puppy can seem overwhelming.

### Location

The best place to start looking is close to home. If you have an emergency, especially one which may be life or death for your Springer, the last thing you want is to have to travel an hour or more to your veterinarian. Being quick to arrive may save your dog's life.

### Cost

Veterinary practices do not follow set fees. They have the ability to be competitive and make up their own prices. In addition, many practices offer deals or price plans to incentivize clients to keep on top of routine checkups. Health plans are not usually insurance based, but they provide vaccines, parasite treatment, and usually money off food and products, for a set monthly cost. This is always an excellent idea to sign up to, as it will help you remember what you must give your dog, as well as save you money.

In addition to this, most practices will have monthly specials to promote certain health aspects. For example, they might have a dental month, where they provide free dental checks and money off dental procedures. Or they may have a lump month, where they provide free lump checks.

## Emergency services

Not all veterinary practices run their own emergency services after-hours. Some contract a specific emergency provider to work for the practice during these times. These after-hours services are usually staffed by veterinarians who specialize in emergency medicine and therefore they are more experienced in critical care in comparison to general practitioners.

**HELPFUL TIP**

Keep Calm and Go to the Vet

There are numerous strategies for keeping your dog calm during trips to the vet's office. One strategy to calm your pet is to use medication or herbal supplements to curb anxious feelings. If your pet is particularly anxious, talk to your vet about available treatment options.

However, for some, continuity is important, and therefore you may find you would prefer to have a veterinarian who does their own after-hours work. While they might not be as experienced, they are likely to create a more calming environment for you and your Springer if an emergency arises in the middle of the night.

## Specialties

Some veterinary practices employ certificate holders to work for them on either a contractual basis or as permanent staff. This is very beneficial, as it means that some veterinary practices will be able to deal with more complicated cases within their own clinic, rather than refer to a veterinary hospital. Certificate holders usually specialize in subjects such as ophthalmology, orthopedics, dermatology, and cardiology.

For some, the idea of being referred to a hospital is not a bad thing, as a large hospital will have specialist equipment and be set up for difficult cases which require hospitalization. For others, the idea of being able to promptly see a specialist vet within their own practice is a major bonus, so that they don't need to take their dog far away or wait for a referral appointment.

## Additional businesses

Some veterinary practices have additional businesses running from their site. These might include boarding kennels, a grooming parlor, hydrotherapy, and puppy training classes. This means that your Springer won't necessarily associate going to the vet with seeing a vet, which may help with their sensitive nature.

# Vaccinations

All dogs should be routinely vaccinated. There are many people in the world who are anti-vaccine campaigners, but there is a wealth of scientific evidence to prove that vaccines are safe and vital for the health of your dog. If you are adamant that you do not wish to vaccinate your dog regularly, then the next best option is to allow your puppy to have his starter vaccine course, then perform a blood test every year to ensure his immunity is sufficiently high. If it is not, then you can vaccinate as a one-off, to boost the immunity he is lacking.

Assuming, though, that vaccines are going to become part of your annual routine for your Springer, he will need a vaccine course at 8-12 weeks old, and then annual booster injections. The initial vaccine course will vary depending on the vaccine brand your vet uses, but usually it will consist of an injection at 8 weeks old, then again 3-4 weeks later. In addition, you may choose to get your dog vaccinated against rabies and kennel cough, which are important in areas where there is a high density of dogs, or where rabies is endemic.

The following diseases are vaccinated against in dogs:

- Distemper = This disease is a virus which can be devastating. It can cause symptoms which are non-specific, such as sneezing, vomiting, and coughing. It can also cause hardening and thickening of the pads on the paws and of the nose. It rapidly progresses to death.

- Parvovirus = This is also a virus which typically affects young puppies. It causes bloody diarrhea, which is extremely contagious. This gradually causes puppies to fade due to dehydration and blood loss.

- Leptospirosis = This disease is a bacterium with several serotypes. Different vaccines cover different serotypes, so you should inquire which vaccine your vet uses. Leptospirosis causes failure of the kidneys and liver, and the most common symptom is yellowing of the gums and eyes, known as jaundice. Some dogs also display neurological symptoms.

- Hepatitis = This is a virus, otherwise known as canine adenovirus, which like distemper causes some vague symptoms. Commonly seen are fatigue, fever, vomiting, diarrhea, and jaundice, and it will rapidly lead to death.

- Parainfluenza = This is sometimes contained in the injection which combines the four above diseases, or it can be part of the kennel cough vaccine. Parainfluenza is a virus, which can lead to a debilitating cough.

- Kennel cough = This is a vaccine which contains Bordetella and Parainfluenza. Together they create a complex disease known as kennel cough. It is highly contagious and causes a honking cough and a fever. This vaccine is squirted up the nose rather than injected.

- **Rabies** = This injection should be given as standard to any dog which lives in a rabies endemic area. It is a dangerous disease which causes aggression, hypersalivation, and neurological symptoms, which lead to death. If a rabid dog bites a human, they also may contract the fatal disease.

# Microchipping

In the UK, microchipping is a legal requirement of all dogs. This law has not yet reached the USA; however, it is still an excellent idea to get your puppy microchipped as soon as you get him. Some breeders will already have done this for you, but if not, you can get your puppy microchipped when he first goes for his initial vaccine course.

A microchip is a small piece of metal that is inserted in between the shoulder blades via means of an injection. It is roughly the size of a grain of rice, and when a scanner is passed over it, it provides a unique number. This number is then registered with a central database company, which stores all the details for registered microchips. If you were to phone the central company and relay the number, they could tell you the name of the owner and contact details of that dog.

Microchipping is a failsafe way of ensuring that your dog can always be traced back to you if he is lost. He cannot lose a microchip, and it is uncommon that they malfunction. The only thing that you must remember is to keep your details up to date with the microchip company. If you move or change your cell phone number, then make sure to tell the microchip company.

# Neutering

Whether or not you neuter your dog is a personal preference; however, there are many health benefits to doing so. With that being said, if you intend to show your Springer Spaniel, you will be required to keep him or her entire.

Neutering a male is called castration, and for a female it is called a spay. The castration procedure is very simple. It requires a short anesthetic, and your dog will be in and out of the vet practice within half a day. Castration ensures that your dog does not wander off looking for females while out on a walk. It also eliminates the risk of testicular and prostate tumors, and decreases the chances of a syndrome called benign prostatic hypertrophy, which is when the prostate enlarges so much that your dog might struggle to urinate and defecate.

A spay procedure on the other hand is a slightly more complicated operation. Nevertheless, your dog will be in and out of the vet's office within a day. The vet may choose to remove just the ovaries, or he may remove the ovaries and the uterus. Both operations will yield the same result, and it is down to the experience of your veterinarian with what he prefers to perform. Spaying your female dog will ensure she does not contract a life-threatening infection of the uterus, called a pyometra. These are extremely common, and very dangerous. Also, if you spay your dog before her second season, it significantly reduces the risk of mammary cancers later in life, as they are influenced by hormones, in particular estrogen and progesterone. If you spay your dog before her first season, the risk is almost non-existent for mammary tumors; however, with this runs the risk of creating a slack urethral sphincter. This is the muscle which closes the exit to the bladder, and its tone is directly related to how much estrogen your dog has come into contact with in her life. Therefore, if you spay your dog before her first season, she will not have ever had estrogen in her body, and she may develop urinary incontinence later in life because of it. Luckily, this can easily be managed with a daily medication. Spaying will also eliminate the risk of ovarian and uterine cancers.

# Internal Parasites

Just as you should routinely treat for external parasites, as discussed in the grooming chapter, you should also routinely treat for internal parasites. These parasites include roundworms and tapeworms.

Some flea treatments also include worming treatments, so one application of a medication will cover all types of parasites, but you should follow your vet's recommendations about what treatments to use on your dog.

Comprehensive worming treatments against roundworms and tapeworms are usually recommended every three months if your dog scavenges, or every six months if he doesn't. Therefore, for Springers, you will certainly have to worm every three months! He won't be able to resist putting his nose to the ground after a scent, and gobbling down anything rotten he finds. If you live in an area where lungworms are prevalent, it is actually best to deworm your dog with a roundworm treatment every month, and then with a tapeworm treatment every three months.

# Pet Insurance

When you have a new dog, it is vital to insure him from the get-go. Especially so if you have a pedigree breed, such as an English Springer Spaniel. Veterinary costs can add up to thousands of dollars, and big bills can come suddenly and unexpectedly.

Insuring from a young age is the best idea, as when your dog is older, there will be more exclusions and higher premiums in comparison to if you had first insured him when he was younger.

There are several types of insurance options, and some people will prefer one kind, whereas others will prefer another. Therefore, read the fine print well to understand fully what you are signing up for. The first type of policy is a pot of money per condition per lifetime. For example, you may be covered for $5,000 for a condition, but once you have spent that, he will not be covered for that condition any longer. Another type of policy will cover for higher amounts of money, but after a year, you can no longer claim for that condition. Finally, the most comprehensive policy is a lifetime policy, where you have a certain amount of money you can claim for a condition per year, and after that year, that pot of money is refreshed. Needless to say, each type of policy will vary in terms of annual premiums.

In addition to the type of policy affecting your premium, you will also have a choice of different levels of excess payment. This, along with the type of policy you choose, can help you tailor your pet insurance to a cost which you can afford.

In the end, pet insurance may seem expensive, but it will save you money and worry in the long run, as you will know that your beloved Springer is covered if something unexpected arises. In addition to pet insurance, by routinely providing preventative veterinary medicine to your dog, he will be as happy and healthy as can be, which he will surely be grateful for, if he was able to comprehend what it is all about!

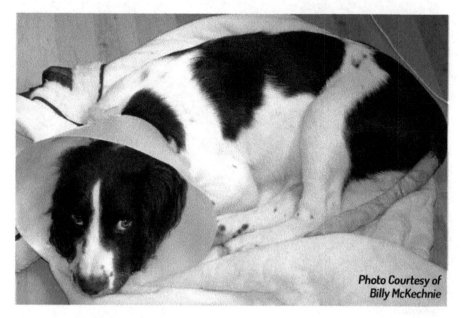

*Photo Courtesy of
Billy McKechnie*

CHAPTER 15
# Diseases and Conditions

English Springer Spaniels, being a pedigree breed, can be prone to certain health conditions during their lifetime. It doesn't mean that your Springer will develop any of these diseases or conditions; however, being on the lookout for them will ensure your dog gets timely and early treatment if any do develop. This chapter will give an overview of the different conditions which English Springer Spaniels have a higher incidence of in comparison to other breeds.

## Hip Dysplasia

The hip joint is a ball and socket joint, where the femur meets the pelvis at the top of the leg. Naturally, the ball at the top of the femur should fit perfectly into the round socket of the pelvis. When a dog has hip dysplasia, the ball and socket do not match up. As a result, the ball slides around in the socket, and in extreme cases, it can luxate out of it.

Hip dysplasia is usually first evident when the dog reaches full size. This is around one to two years old. A dog with hip dysplasia will have a wobbly gait and intermittent lameness, but otherwise seem fine. Unfortunately, if it is not managed from early on, it rapidly progresses to early onset arthritis, which can be debilitating.

Hip dysplasia can be prevented by ensuring that dogs with poor hip scores are not bred from. A hip score can be determined via an X-ray of the joint, which is then sent off to the University of Pennsylvania PennHIP program in the USA, or the Kennel Club in the UK.

Once a dog has developed hip dysplasia, there are two options; conservative management or surgery. In extreme cases, a hip replacement is an option, but that is an expensive and technical procedure. Conservative management, on the other hand, involves plenty of controlled on-leash exercise, limiting jumping and uncontrolled running, hydrotherapy, and physiotherapy, to improve the muscle strength over the hindquarters. Joint supplements containing glucosamine and chondroitin, and a diet which is high in omega oils, will also slow down the onset of arthritis.

# Ear Infections

The beautiful ears of an English Springer Spaniel can unfortunately be prone to ear infections. This is because since the pinna (flap) of the ear folds down, it creates a warm and moist environment within the ear, which is perfect for yeast and bacteria to grow in. In Chapter 13, we discussed the impor-

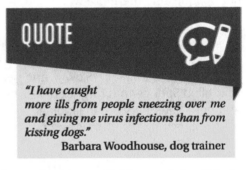

QUOTE

*"I have caught more ills from people sneezing over me and giving me virus infections than from kissing dogs."*
Barbara Woodhouse, dog trainer

tance of ear cleaning, especially after swimming, and this certainly will help reduce the likelihood of an infection.

If your Springer does contract an ear infection, it is likely that he will show signs such as shaking his head and scratching his ears. If it progresses to a more serious infection of the middle ear as well, you might notice a head tilt or loss of balance. Ear infections are extremely sore, and can be serious, so it is important that you take your Springer to a vet promptly. He will likely need medicated ear drops to get on top of the infection. If it has progressed to a middle ear infection, he might be admitted for an ear flush instead or be given oral treatment.

137

# Cataracts

A cataract is a condition of the lens in the eye, where it becomes white and opaque, leading to blindness. The lens is the part of the eye which changes shape to be able to direct the light onto the back of the eye appropriately. If this doesn't work, vision becomes blurry. Cataracts are when the lens starts to become opaque. Some dogs develop them in just one eye, and other dogs develop them bilaterally. Sometimes they can be due to a medical condition, such as diabetes, other times it can be genetic, as is the case for English Springer Spaniels, and finally sometimes it can just be unfortunate luck.

A veterinarian will diagnose cataracts by looking in the eye with an ophthalmoscope. This is a device which shines light in the eye and bounces it back to a magnified glass. If the light shines all the way to the back of the eye, where the retina is, then the lens is normal. However, if the light reflects off the lens instead, then it has developed a cataract.

Nuclear sclerosis, to the naked eye, looks very similar to a cataract. This is a normal condensing of the lens, which happens with age; however, it is not opaque, and therefore with the ophthalmoscope, a vet can look to the very back of the eye.

There is nothing medical that can be done for a cataract, so as they progress, it is worth ensuring that voice commands are well cemented in your Springer's training. "Slowly" and "wait" will become very useful when your blind Springer has forgotten he is blind, and is following a scent on the ground! A veterinary ophthalmologist can replace the lens in a referral hospital setting; however, this is an uncommon operation and requires extensive technical expertise.

# Atopic Dermatitis

Atopic dermatitis, otherwise known as atopy, is an allergic condition of the skin. Usually atopy is caused by environmental allergens, such as pollens or grasses, but sometimes food proteins can also play a role. It causes extremely itchy and reddened skin, usually in the region of the belly, flanks, and underarms. It can also cause the ear canals to become itchy, which looks like an ear infection.

Atopy is frustrating, as it cannot be treated, only managed. There are many options for treatment, which actually suggests that there is not a single treatment which is extremely effective, otherwise everyone would use that one treatment. There are several oral medications available to decrease the itching, but many have side effects, such as increased thirst, urination, and hunger. Antihistamines and immunomodulatory injections are also widely used to variable effect. A diet high in omega oils also seems to have some efficacy in reducing inflammation in the skin, but in the end, most owners end up using a combination of these options, in combination with allergy avoidance, to manage their dog's atopy.

# Phosphofructokinase (PFK) Deficiency

PFK is a genetic disease which results in the metabolism of glucose being defective. As a result, your dog will not be able to produce sufficient energy for his muscles to work properly. This causes the main symptom: exercise intolerance.

PFK also leads to destruction of red blood cells, which causes anemia. The main symptoms of anemia are pale gums and extreme tiredness.

The disease is an autosomal recessive condition, and therefore it is possible for a Springer to be a carrier of the disease, but not show any symptoms or be affected. A carrier, however, can pass on the genes to his or her offspring, so it is important to know the status of your dog before breeding.

There are no treatments which have proven to be effective, so the only way to reduce it is through responsible breeding decisions.

# Canine Fucosidosis

Canine fucosidosis is a neurological disease which specifically affects English Springer Spaniels. It is due to a deficiency of an enzyme called alpha-L-fucosidase. This enzyme is usually active in white blood cells and the plasma in the bloodstream. Without the enzyme, fucose-rich material is stored within the cells of the nervous system. Also, complex carbohydrates are not able to be broken down which have been stored in the cells.

The condition becomes apparent between 18 months and four years of age, and common symptoms include regression of training, behavior changes, blindness, poor balance, loss of hearing, and decreased weight. Sadly, it is almost always fatal, as to date there are no effective treatments.

# Lipomas

Lipomas are common within the English Springer Spaniel breed. Any lumps can appear worrying, as nobody wants to think their dog has cancer, but the good news is lipomas are benign and mainly harmless lumps.

A lipoma develops when a fat cell mutates and replicates uncontrollably. Therefore, the lump is made up of mainly fat. A veterinarian can easily diagnose lipomas through inserting a needle and aspirating a small amount to look at under the microscope. This test is called a fine needle aspirate, and is quick and easy to perform. All lumps should have a fine needle aspirate, as some lumps can feel soft like a lipoma, yet be more sinister; therefore, all lumps should be treated as serious until confirmed otherwise.

Lipomas don't usually need to be surgically removed unless they are present in areas which are causing a restriction in movement, such as near joints. Nevertheless, if they are removed, the surgery is usually simple and quick.

# Mammary Cancer

Mammary cancers can be various in types. The most common ones are carcinomas; however, every type of mammary cancer behaves differently in each dog. Mammary cancers are driven by hormones, such as estrogen and progesterone. These can be prevented from ever entering the blood stream by spaying your female dog prior to her first season. This is not usually the first line option for spaying, however, as estrogen helps to tighten up the urethral sphincter at the exit of the bladder, so if a dog has never had estrogen in her body, she may leak urine. Therefore, the pros and cons need to be weighed.

The main sign of mammary cancer is a lump behind or near the teat. It can be soft or hard, round or a strange shape, mobile or fixed, and red or skin colored. In other words, there is not a set way that a mammary cancer lump will look. They quickly progress to the neighboring mammary glands, as well as the lymph nodes at the end of each mammary strip.

To confirm a diagnosis, a fine needle aspirate will indicate what sort of lump it is; however, surgical removal and examination by a laboratory is important to make sure whether it needs to be followed up with chemotherapy.

# Diabetes Mellitus

Diabetes mellitus is a disease of the pancreas. The pancreas has several types of cells in it which produce insulin and glucagon. These are chemical indicators for cells in the body to either uptake glucose out of the blood, to store or use, and therefore decrease the blood sugar levels, or alternatively tell the body to release stored glucose into the blood, to increase blood sugar levels.

When a dog has diabetes, the insulin production is deficient. Insulin is the chemical indicator which decreases blood sugar levels, and therefore a dog with diabetes has a constantly high amount of glucose running around his body. This can lead to ketones being produced from the glucose, which can cause neurological symptoms and make your dog feel very ill.

In addition, high glucose levels can cause cataracts, a change in appetite, and added pressure on internal organs. Diabetes can be controlled through twice daily injections with insulin at the time of breakfast and dinner, so that the blood sugar levels do not peak after a meal. Unfortunately, there is no cure for diabetes, and to ensure treatment is fully effective, your dog will require your dedication to treatment. However, once under control, a diabetic dog can live a completely normal life.

# Hepatitis

Chronic hepatitis is a condition which older English Springer Spaniels are prone to developing. It is when the liver becomes inflamed and liver cells gradually begin to die off.

There can be many infectious and cancerous causes of hepatitis, so all hepatitis cases should be thoroughly investigated; however, the condition in Springer Spaniels usually ends up being idiopathic, meaning the origin of the condition is unknown.

Symptoms of hepatitis include abdominal pain, depression, disorientation, a pot-belly, increased thirst, increased urination, jaundice, a decreased appetite, weight loss, vomiting, a poor coat, and seizures. A dog with hepatitis may have all of these, or just one or two, and therefore since these symptoms are not very specific, the disease can be confused with many other conditions in the beginning.

Diagnosis is based initially on a blood test, and then further investigation is usually performed via ultrasound imaging. The vet may also take a liver biopsy to understand the architecture of the liver and the health status of the liver cells.

Treatment for liver disease is mainly aimed at stopping further progression, as well as reducing strain on the liver. Initially, this may require your Springer to be hospitalized to receive intravenous fluids to flush out the system. After this, various ongoing oral medications are available, and your dog will also require a diet change. Hepatitis diets are low in protein quantity, and high in protein quality, so that the liver does not need to process as much protein to still provide the body with the same amount.

# Epilepsy

Epilepsy is a condition of the brain, which first becomes apparent between one and five years of age, and causes both full and partial seizures. A full seizure is what most people typically know, which is when your dog loses the ability to control himself, and may fall to the floor, shake, salivate, have stiff legs, and defecate or urinate. This lasts for 30 seconds to a few minutes, and during this time, he cannot be distracted. You might also notice a subtle change in behavior in the hours prior to and following the seizure.

Partial seizures can also happen. These manifest as abnormal neurological behaviors, which your dog cannot control, and might include an area of regional twitching, shaking, or fly-snapping behavior.

Both partial and full seizures are caused by nerves within the brain becoming hyperexcitable, and all firing electrical impulses at the same time. While epilepsy can appear scary, a dog with epilepsy can live a completely normal life. There are excellent medications, which need to be given daily and which significantly reduce the incidence of seizures, often reducing them from weekly or monthly, to yearly. Seizure medications are metabolized by the liver, and therefore, if your dog has liver disease or is older, careful monitoring must take place, with blood tests every six months.

If your dog is having many seizures, one after another, or a seizure which lasts more than five minutes, it is very important that he urgently sees a vet. These types of seizures can cause starvation of oxygen to the brain, and are not usually caused by epilepsy. Also, if your Springer is having seizures for the first time, but he is old, then this is also unlikely to be epilepsy, as epilepsy usually begins from a young age.

While the list of Springer Spaniel diseases may seem long, it should not be off-putting. Springers can be extremely healthy dogs and never manifest any of these diseases in their lifetime, especially if the one you purchase has been bred by a responsible breeder. Nevertheless, it is important to be prepared, both in knowledge and with pet insurance, so that if you notice any medical condition with your Springer Spaniel, it can be treated early on to ensure your Springer's health does not deteriorate further.

Photo Courtesy of
Lise Sallaup

# CHAPTER 16
# Hunting

Hunting may not be for every English Springer Spaniel owner; however, hunting plays a big role in the genetics of the breed. The working Springer has its roots firmly embedded in the hunting world, and while the breed is now used for far more than hunting, as discussed in the next chapter, you cannot go wrong with using a working Springer Spaniel in the field.

The English Springer Spaniel is a versatile hunting dog, successful for hunting both ground birds, known as upland hunting, and water birds. His enthusiasm, trainability, and drive make him an excellent hunting companion. If you are new to hunting, then an English Springer Spaniel is a good choice.

# Upland Hunting

Upland hunting may include several different types of birds, such as pheasants, grouse, quail, and partridges. A dog is needed for upland hunting because these birds often live in dense undergrowth, and therefore are difficult to find and flush without the use of a dog.

Springer Spaniels are excellent dogs for flushing these types of birds. They generally work in close proximity to the hunter, so it is important that they are responsive to voice or whistle commands to ensure they do not come to any harm.

Springer Spaniels meet their work with enthusiasm, and there is nothing better than sending them out on the search for a bird, seeing their tail exuberantly wag from side to side, often with their whole bottom following, with their nose to the ground doing the job. This enthusiasm can both help and hinder your hunt if you do not train your Springer well, as Springers can easily lock exclusively onto the trail of a bird, becoming unresponsive to their master as they focus solely on the delights of the smell.

Once the bird is flushed into the air, the hunter will shoot it. It is then the Springer's job to find the shot bird and retrieve it for his master without damaging it.

# Waterfowl Hunting

Less commonly, Springer Spaniels may be used for waterfowl hunting. This type of hunting with a dog requires the dog to perform a slightly different task from upland hunting. Waterfowl hunting does not require the Springer to flush out birds, but instead he will just have the role of collecting from the water.

This is a job which a Springer can do well, as they have a double coat which keeps them insulated in the water. That, coupled with their magnetic pull to the water, will see them collecting birds all day with enthusiasm.

Photo Courtesy of
Andrew MacVicar

Waterfowl hunting, however, will commonly not use Springers, and instead use larger Retriever breeds of dogs. This is because Springers may be competent at bringing back a duck, but if a goose is shot, they will struggle to retrieve such a big bird from the water. That doesn't mean they won't try though, as they are always keen to please.

## Selecting a Puppy for Hunting

Your gundog puppy should come from a working Springer Spaniel breeder, rather than a show Springer Spaniel breeder. That way you can determine that he will have the drive and energy to do the job. Working Springer breeders are likely to select the parents specifically for their excellent working traits, so you might already be aware of certain working dogs which excel in the area.

When visiting the puppies, you should ask whether they have had any exposure to gunshots already. Some breeders will hunt on their land, so hearing gunshots is an everyday part of life. Early exposure will ensure there are no phobias in the future.

As you view the litter, there are a few things to look out for, to ensure you pick a puppy which is excellent for hunting. Start by observing the puppies in their environment. Look out for their individual characters. You want a bold puppy, but not the most dominant, and one which is friendly. So take note if there's one that takes a particular liking to you.

Observe that the puppy runs straight and has good bone to his legs. His tail is most likely to be docked, as this will stop him injuring it in the field, but you want one which hasn't got his tail docked too short, as the tail is a good indicator in the field of what the nose is discovering. One-third in length is a good length for a docked tail.

Next, ask the breeder some questions. How have the parents fared in action or in field trials? What type of hunting have they done? Have they had health checks, and are they free from any hereditary diseases? You should ask to see the paperwork of both the parents, as well as the puppies, to ensure they are properly registered.

Finally, just trust your instincts. If there is a puppy you feel particularly drawn to, many people believe this is a positive indicator. There is a lot of merit in the saying "your puppy will choose you."

# Gundog Training

The type of training you put your time and effort into depends very much on the type of hunting you wish to do. Upland hunting is notoriously harsh, with the use of choke chains and stern training. Springers have a sensitive nature, and do not respond well to this type of training, and therefore, a little more patience and a kinder approach will ensure that you get off to a good start with upland hunting. You may reap the rewards a bit later than with a traditionally trained upland hunting dog, but you will foster a much better working relationship with your Springer Spaniel and have a much more enjoyable time out in the field.

Photo Courtesy of
Claudia Bruhn

Voice and whistle commands are important when upland hunting. There are three main commands which must be firmly in place before you use your Springer Spaniel in the field: "come," "sit," and "turn." "Come" is usually taught as both a voice command and a long blow on the whistle. It is easy to teach and should be the foundation of all hunting training. You can start recall training as soon as you bring your puppy home, and some tips for teaching this command are given in Chapter 7. If you cannot call your Springer off of a smell, then you do not have control over him, which is dangerous when it involves guns. The next command which is important is "sit." This is both a safety command and a convenience. The command is actually a blend of "sit" and "stay," both taught earlier in Chapter 9, and your Springer should not get up until released. Finally, the third vital command is "turn." This is given by two toots on a whistle. This command is vital for when your Springer is running around trying to flush out birds which are out of your gun range and you want him to come back toward you. His job is useless if the birds he flushes are not within range.

Waterfowl hunting, on the other hand, is slightly less harsh than upland hunting training. This because the dogs should not be out in front of the hunter when he is shooting, so unlike upland hunting, the dog should never be in the line of fire. There are two ways to train a waterfowl hunting dog. The first is to break (collect) as soon as the bird drops. This enables him to locate the bird immediately, and with little effort, and it also ensures the bird is collected promptly in case he has just been badly injured and not killed. The downside to this is that your Springer will become so enthusiastic that he may start anticipating the gunshot, and break the second he hears the noise, rather than when the bird falls. This in turn is likely to disturb all the birds and slow the hunt down. The other way you can train your water-fowl hunting dog is to only break once you command him. He should sit and stay waiting until given the command to go and collect. Then he will go and find the birds one by one, which are floating on the water after being shot.

Initially, when training is still in the early days, you may teach him to seek and retrieve a dummy bird. This is the best way to introduce your Springer to hunting, whether it be upland or waterfowl hunting.

So, whether you decide to professionally hunt with your Spaniel, hunt as a hobby, or simply take your Spaniel regularly out into the countryside, he will certainly enjoy every second he has, following the smell of birds and wildlife. As this chapter has highlighted, having sound training in place will ensure it is an enjoyable experience for all, and that your Spaniel is able to control his enthusiasm.

Photo Courtesy of
Graham Briggs

Photo Courtesy of
Lise Sallaup

# CHAPTER 17
# Working Dogs

Previous chapters have discussed the English Springer Spaniel's two-thousand-year history as a working dog, and how the working strain has only recently diverged from the show strain. However, the Springer Spaniel is by nature a dog with a job to do. Chapter 16 discussed the role of the working Springer as a hunting dog, but in the modern world, the adaptable Springer Spaniel is able to exercise his talents in many more areas than just the field.

The key to his success as a modern working dog is his intelligence, trainability, temperament, stamina, and most importantly his remarkable sense of smell.

Springers may be bred specifically for a role in a particular field, or they may come from a rescue environment. Maybe they have not been able to settle into family life, but they have an abundance of energy and drive, making them suitable for training in another field. For this reason, it is often the dogs from working lines that will be seen in search and rescue, alongside police handlers, or at ports and airports, whereas the quieter show lines may find their vocation as assistance dogs.

# Search and Rescue

The working Springer Spaniel is ideally suited to search and rescue, as not only is his sensitive nose well equipped for following a scent, but he also has the stamina and tough athleticism necessary for working over challenging terrains. He is also double coated to keep him warm in extreme conditions.

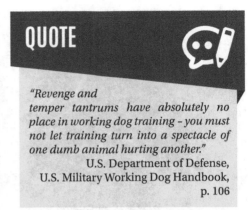

**QUOTE**

*"Revenge and temper tantrums have absolutely no place in working dog training – you must not let training turn into a spectacle of one dumb animal hurting another."*
U.S. Department of Defense,
U.S. Military Working Dog Handbook,
p. 106

Springer Spaniels are often favored over the more commonly seen German Shepherds for search and rescue for the simple reason that they are less threatening. Apart from walkers who have lost their way or met with an injury, they are quite often employed to search for vulnerable people, such as missing children, individuals intent on self-harm, or elderly people with dementia who have wandered away from home. Such individuals could be frightened to be confronted with a German Shepherd, but the sight of a friendly English Springer Spaniel may defuse an otherwise fraught situation.

*Photo Courtesy of Claudia Bruhn*

*Photo Courtesy of Billy McKechnie*

Spaniels used in search and rescue are trained to recognize human scent, and to bark when they find someone. They will then return to their handler, running back and forth between the handler and the missing person until they are found.

In 2017, the fire services department in Hong Kong acquired three Springer Spaniels from the UK named Jack, Judy, and Spike to replace their aging Labrador Retrievers. Springer Spaniels were chosen because their smaller size enabled them to gain access to scrubby areas and places in the mountains that could not be reached on foot.

English Springer Spaniels used in search and rescue are not always owned and trained by an official body. Individual owners can train with the National Search and Rescue Dog Association in their country, gain official qualifications, and join their local mountain or lowland rescue teams. This is a heavy commitment, but very rewarding for those who feel drawn to search and rescue, and own a suitable dog.

# Forensics

Springer Spaniels frequently play a key role in forensic investigation because of their acutely sensitive sense of smell.

Humans typically have 5 million olfactory receptors in the nasal cavity, which are cells dedicated to smell. Springer Spaniels have 300 million. In addition, they have four times the brain power specifically devoted to processing scents. This means that they can pick out individual ingredients within a cocktail of scents. Coupled with this ability, the Springer Spaniel is also highly trainable, so their talents may be put to use in detecting specific scents that no man or machine could pick out, making them uniquely valuable in the field of forensics.

## Crime scene

Springer Spaniels may typically be used at the scene of a crime to detect blood, or cadaverine, which is a fluid emitted soon after death by an animal or human body. Detection dogs can pick up the most minute traces of these compounds, invisible to the naked eye. By homing in on a specific area, forensic teams can then take samples for DNA testing. So, while a dog's reaction alone is not enough to secure a conviction, further testing of areas identified by the dog may produce the evidence that can solve a case beyond any reasonable doubt.

Often, dogs used for detection at crime scenes are trained to identify one specific marker. For example, a certain dog may detect only blood, while another may detect only cadaverine. And the way they communicate to the handler may be by barking at the spot where they pick up the scent, or by pointing. A dog trained in more than one scent may mark in different ways.

Sammy the Springer Spaniel is a crime scene detection dog for the South Wales Fire and Rescue Service. He is trained to detect whether an accelerant has been used in a suspected case of arson. Sammy can pick up traces of inflammable fluids up to two weeks after a blaze, and he indicates their presence by staring at the specific spot. Crime scene investigators then take samples for further investigation.

Tweed the Springer Spaniel is a digital device detection dog working with Devon and Cornwall Police in England. Criminals often go to great lengths to hide incriminating digital storage devices such as USB sticks, SD cards, hard drives, and mobile devices, which can be located much more effectively by use of a dog's sense of smell than by a human search.

Photo Courtesy of Charles Phillips

## Customs & Excise

Springer Spaniels are popular within the field of customs and border patrol, as they are working in close proximity to the general public, so their non-threatening nature makes them a more acceptable presence in ports, airports, and railway stations. They are also smaller than German Shepherds, which makes them more suited to working in confined spaces.

Rather than reacting in an excitable way, which is less appropriate in a public environment, they are often trained to indicate with a passive alert. That is to say, they will sit quietly in front of the object.

Springer Spaniels working in customs and border patrol will typically be trained to detect the presence of narcotics, tobacco, explosives, firearms, animal products, currency, and electronics. Their acutely sensitive sense of smell can pick out the target even when it has been deliberately masked by something else; for example, drugs concealed in coffee. In some parts of the world, Springer Spaniels will be used to sniff out illegal ivory, rhino horn, or other animal products poached from endangered species. They are therefore on the frontline of world wildlife conservation.

Polly the Springer Spaniel was rescued from an animal shelter in 2001, and became a detector dog for UK Customs. During her career, she sniffed out more than £3 million in cash, 540kg of cannabis, 68kg of ecstasy, and 500g of amphetamine. Her biggest find was £1.3 million concealed in a false floor of a truck. She also confounded expectations by detecting £50,000 concealed in the running wheel of a car, something thought to be impossible.

## Combat & terrorism

Springer Spaniels will often be found in areas of conflict, or entering into dangerous situations where their acute sense of smell is put to work sniffing out explosives. It takes a special kind of Springer Spaniel to enter these highly charged environments, and trainers look for bold and confident dogs that remain focused and unafraid in challenging surroundings.

The British Army actually has Military Working Dog Regiments to provide trained dogs and handlers. Dogs killed in action are buried with full military honors, and dogs can also be awarded medals. In 2012, a Springer Spaniel named Theo was posthumously awarded the PDSA Dickin Medal, the animal equivalent of the Victoria Cross, for setting a record for bomb finds in Afghanistan during deployment with his handler, Lance Corporal Liam Tasker. As a measure of the bond between dog and handler, when Liam Tasker was killed by a sniper in 2011, Theo died of a seizure within hours.

Scooby the Springer served in Afghanistan, Iraq, Kosovo, and Bosnia. When employed in Jordan on Operation Shamal Storm, he wore specially designed combat gear, with goggles, ear muffs, and desert boots. Far from a fashion statement, this protective clothing enabled him to perform his demanding job in the environment in which he found himself.

# Assistance Dogs

English Springer Spaniels can also be found at work in more domestic environments, where their trainability and friendly nature can enable people with medical conditions to live their lives to the full. Springers are happy dogs with a loving and caring disposition, and just being around them can make a real difference. So without any specific training at all, they can lift the spirits of people suffering from depression, they can communicate in a unique way with adults and children with autism and Asperger's syndrome, they can engage with the sick and elderly, and bring their special blend of warmth and optimism into the lives of all sorts of people who are facing challenges to their physical or mental health.

Springers have even been employed within the medical world to detect cancers before any symptoms are apparent. A recent example is a Springer Spaniel that was able to detect lung cancer in a sufferer's breath. And in Vancouver General Hospital in Canada, a Springer Spaniel named Angus has been trained to sniff out the superbug Clostridium difficile, with the potential to save many lives.

When it comes to assistance dogs, most people will think immediately of guide dogs for the blind. Springer Spaniels are not used in this capacity as they are too exuberant by nature, but that is not to say they can't play an important role in other areas.

## Hearing dogs for the deaf

Springer Spaniels are not one of the most common breeds used as hearing dogs for the deaf; Cocker Spaniels are preferred. However, they are sometimes found in this valuable role.

Hearing dogs are trained to alert their deaf owners to sounds such as the doorbell or telephone. They may react to the oven buzzer, the baby's cry, and vitally, the smoke alarm. When they react to an alert, they will nudge their owner and lead them to the source of the sound.

Hearing dogs enable their owners to achieve a greater degree of independence and personal safety, but they also offer companionship, as living with a disability can feel very isolating.

Although many Springer Spaniels get on well as hearing dogs for the deaf, it didn't suit Bruno. Bruno had to return twice to the Beatrice Wright Centre in Yorkshire, England, for refresher training, but he just couldn't let go of his chase instincts, which he found far more compelling than the treats on offer to come back. However, the team had faith in Bruno, and his cheeky, sociable nature made him an ideal candidate to be an applicant assessment dog. In his new role, Bruno helped with the induction process for new clients as they learned how to live with a hearing dog. So even if a Springer Spaniel doesn't make the grade in one capacity, sensitive reassessment of his skills can enable him to be a star in another role.

## Epilepsy & diabetes

In the case of epilepsy and diabetes, sufferers live normal lives, but this may be interrupted by a seizure in the case of epilepsy, or abnormal blood sugar levels in the case of diabetes which can lead to unconsciousness.

In both cases, there will be warning indicators of an impending attack that will be undetectable by other people, even the sufferer themselves. But the super sensitivity of an alert dog can detect and raise the alarm, so that appropriate measures can be taken.

In the case of epilepsy, a seizure alert dog is trained to provide a warning up to 50 minutes before the seizure occurs, allowing the sufferer to find a place of safety and privacy. This is potentially life-saving, and it also gives people with epilepsy the confidence to lead an independent life.

In the case of diabetes, a diabetes alert dog can detect the scent of their owner's rapidly dropping blood sugar level, which is called

Photo Courtesy of Megan Wharrie

hypoglycemia. They will then nudge them or bark, prompting them to take glucose or have a sugary drink. The dog's early alert can prevent unconsciousness. Diabetes alert dogs can also detect if their owner's blood sugar is dangerously high, which can lead to serious health complications, so the owner knows in this case to inject with insulin.

Jess the Springer Spaniel is a diabetes alert dog for her six-year-old master, Jac, who lives in Wales. Jess was already the family dog before Jac developed type 1 diabetes, and was trained by the family to fulfill this vital role. When Jac's blood sugar spikes or dips, Jess retrieves a testing kit. This demonstrates that to be an alert dog, all that is needed is the nose, devotion, and intelligence of a Springer Spaniel.

Springer Spaniels are such individuals that there is never a one-size-fits-all vocation for such a personality-packed breed. However, what can be said is that they are all highly intelligent, with finely tuned physical talents as well as their natural companionable nature. Springer Spaniels have all the attributes to rise to modern-day challenges, and excel both in doing a job that no human could do as successfully, and brightening their working environment in a way that only a Springer Spaniel can.

# CHAPTER 18
# Living with a Senior Dog

As with every living being on the Earth, aging is a natural and inevitable process. Age is just a number, and not a disease in itself; however, the older your Springer Spaniel becomes, the more likely he will develop some age-related ailments. Nevertheless, there are plenty of things you can do to manage the health and welfare of your older Springer, so that he can live comfortably into his twilight years.

## Diet

Diet is an excellent place to start when it comes to managing the health of your elderly dog. A senior English Springer Spaniel is defined as one that is eight years old or older. Any dog in this age bracket should be transitioned onto a senior dog food diet.

Senior diets are slightly different from diets for younger dogs. The calories are usually slightly less than a diet for younger dogs, as senior dogs are more sedentary. At least, for most breeds that is applicable, but Springer Spaniels tend to think they are able to be on the go until the day they die. Also,

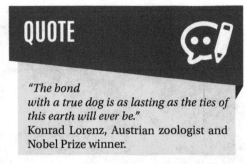

**QUOTE**

*"The bond with a true dog is as lasting as the ties of this earth will ever be."*
Konrad Lorenz, Austrian zoologist and Nobel Prize winner.

the nutrient quantities differ from those in younger dog food, as the nutrients are no longer needed for growth.

In addition to different nutrient and calorie quantities, senior foods usually contain higher quantities of omega fatty acids, in particular omega-3 and omega-6. These promote healthy joint, coat, skin, heart, and brain health, all of which are vital in older dogs.

Senior food may also contain joint supplements such as glucosamine and chondroitin. These are compounds which stimulate the synthesis of glycosaminoglycans, the building blocks of cartilage. These are what deteriorate in the joints as they get older and the joints develop arthritis.

If your Springer Spaniel has had poor dental hygiene during his life, there may come a point in his senior years where he has missing teeth, and those that remain are ground down to the gum. Even at an advanced age, dental care can improve your dog's oral comfort considerably. But in some cases, your dog may no longer be able to manage dry kibble, in which case it is beneficial to soak it first, or move gradually to a soft senior dog food.

## Senior Wellness Checks

Part of routine veterinary care for elderly patients includes regular senior wellness checks. These are checks at the veterinary clinic, usually yearly, to investigate the general health of your senior Springer. Your vet will check the teeth for dental disease, heart for heart murmurs, lungs for fibrosis, abdomen for the size of the liver and kidneys, and finally the joints for any creaking or reduced range of motion.

He might also do a simple test to check your dog's blood pressure. This is done by placing a cuff around your dog's leg which inflates, and then the pulse is listened for further down the leg as it is deflated.

*Photo Courtesy of
Trevor Kerr
www.trevkerrphotographer.com*

Your vet is also likely to take blood to analyze. This way, you can ensure your Springer's general organ health is good, especially the liver. As we discussed in Chapter 15, English Springer Spaniels can be prone to developing hepatitis.

# Arthritis

Arthritis is a condition of the joints. It occurs when the cartilage of the joints degrades, and the joint fluid becomes thin and full of inflammatory factors. It is very sore, and the main symptom is stiffness arising from rest after exercise. Lameness can also be apparent if your dog has arthritis on just one side. It is common for Springer Spaniels to develop arthritis when they are older, as even if they do not have hip dysplasia, as discussed in Chapter 15, they are extremely active dogs who run and jump and put a lot of stress on their joints throughout their lives.

Arthritis cannot be reversed or cured, but the progression can be slowed down. There are also excellent pain relief options to manage the discomfort that it brings. In addition to pain relief medications, omega fatty acids can provide anti-inflammatory properties when fed in the correct quantities. Omega-3 and omega-6 should be in a ratio of 1:3. As discussed earlier, joint supplements can also be very beneficial if they have not already been added to the diet.

Other options to improve the comfort of your arthritic Springer include weight management, physiotherapy, hydrotherapy, and acupuncture. You should not pick and choose when it comes to management modalities, as you will get the best effect when you use a combination of management options.

Practical considerations that may help your arthritic Springer in his senior years may include a ramp for getting into and out of the car, an orthopedic dog bed, and a coat for cold weather to keep his back and joints warm.

# Dementia

Many people do not realize that dogs can get dementia too, although it is not called dementia in dogs; it is known as canine cognitive dysfunction, or CCD. CCD is a degenerative process of the brain, which leads to dullness and lethargy. Some owners also notice a behavior change or unusual behaviors, such as urinating in the house or aimless wandering.

CCD can be managed with some excellent medication which improves the blood flow to the brain. This allows extra oxygen to reach the brain which helps the brain cells work more effectively, giving a new lease of life for your Springer.

# Organ Deterioration

During the lifetime of any dog, the kidneys and liver are two organs which work extremely hard to filter out and remove waste products from the body. As a result, they can start to deteriorate in your dog's senior years.

Symptoms may include loss of appetite, vomiting, drinking more, and urinating more. In addition to this, liver disease may cause jaundice, which presents as yellow gums, and kidney disease may cause anemia, which presents as pale gums. Your veterinarian will investigate the health of your Springer's internal organs through a blood test, and if he is concerned, may carry out an ultrasound examination.

There are excellent diets available for management of kidney disease and liver disease in older dogs, which is the main method of treatment. This reduces pressure on them to work hard to filter out waste products. In addition to that, there are medications available to help improve the efficiency of the organs, which a veterinarian will be able to dispense.

# Loss of Senses

When a dog ages, so does their sight and hearing. Not all dogs go deaf and/or blind; however, preparing for it will make your life easier when trying to control your senior Springer. Deafness and blindness will not slow down your Springer, as he will easily adapt, but it can bring with it some dangers, such as getting lost or not having any recall in dangerous situations.

For blindness, reinforcing voice commands will aid in controlling your dog. You can also introduce new voice commands such as stop, wait, and step. These should ideally be done before your dog goes completely blind.

*Photo Courtesy of Julie Hoffman*

For deafness, hand commands are very useful, such as the forward-facing palm of your hand for sit, and pointing to the ground for lie down. When you are in public spaces or places where your dog can run off, keeping him on a long training lead will stop him from causing a nuisance, or worse, coming into danger.

# Bladder Control

Loss of bladder control can be upsetting for both your dog and yourself. Not only will it require extensive cleaning of your house, but also your Springer will need some help maintaining their own personal hygiene, as excessive urine leakage can lead to scalding around the hindquarters.

Urine leakage is usually a problem of female dogs which have been spayed before their first season, which is more common in English Springer Spaniels than other breeds, since by doing this you are decreasing the chances of developing mammary cancer.

Another reason why your elderly dog may start experiencing loss of bladder control is because of arthritis or spondylosis of the back. This can impinge on the spinal cord, affecting the nerves which innervate the bladder and the urethral sphincter, which closes it.

Luckily there are excellent medications which help control the bladder by improving muscle tone of the sphincter and lining of the bladder. These must be taken daily, but they are well tolerated and the results are generally very good.

# Saying Goodbye

For most owners who have a pet which has reached senior age, there will come a day when they have to make a decision to say goodbye and put their pet to sleep. You may be overwhelmed by this decision when you get to this stage, which is a completely normal feeling, as the decision is a heavy one to make.

Nevertheless, while it isn't an easy decision, the fact that you can decide to end the ongoing suffering of your Springer Spaniel, when his quality of life has deteriorated to a very low point, is actually a last favor that you can give your beloved friend.

A veterinarian will carry out the procedure, either in the vet practice or at your home. It is a simple overdose injection of an anesthetic. This results in exactly what is expected by the name—your dog will fall into a deep sleep, and quietly and peacefully slip away. It is completely painless. Afterward, you might notice some twitching, voiding of the bladder or bowels, or a deep breath. This is because after a dog has passed away, when the muscles shut down, they initially contract. It doesn't mean that the injection hasn't worked.

It is never easy to make the decision, and after a lifetime of Springer Spaniel joy, you are sure to feel major heartache. But you should try to take the opportunity to remember all the happy times you have had throughout your life together, and how grateful you are to have had your life blessed with them for so many years.

Photo Courtesy of
Louise Stewart